Celebrating
Step Back from the Baggage Claim

"Jason, and this book, aspire to make a difference - and are doing so as more and more people put this spirit into action in their organizations. He offers valuable reminders and simple principles that can guide the leadership actions you take in your own life and business."
- Howard Behar, *former President*, **Starbucks Coffee**

"*Step Back from the Baggage Claim* is a must read for anyone interested in excelling at international business. Too often your managers are looking for an elegant solution or for the 'silver bullet' to doing business effectively. However, Jason's book covers the key soft aspects to gaining cooperation in a cross-cultural and cross-national business world. I recommend this book for anyone interested in international business."
- P. Roberto Garcia, Ph.D, *Professor of International Business and Co-Director of the Supply Chain and Global Management Academy*, Indiana University, **Kelley School of Business**

"To *Step Back from the Baggage Claim* means to exit the rat race, if only for a moment. This disciplined practice creates the space, a kind of opening that allows us to observe our blind spots, home to our hidden assumptions and taken for granted presuppositions. In the act of 'stepping back,' we make room for new ways of being and thinking, allowing our best selves and our best leadership to emerge."
- Dr. Wiley "Chip" Souba, *Dean*, **Dartmouth Medical School**

The *Step Back Movement* has been highlighted by:

* *The New York Times* * *International Herald Tribune*
* *Kiplinger* * *National Geographic Traveler* * *Book TV*
* *ABC News* * *Seattle Times* * and many more...

www.StepBackFromTheBaggageClaim.com

Step Back from the Baggage Claim
Change the World, Start at the Airport
BUSINESS LEADER EDITION

**Copyright 2008, 2010 - revised Business Leader Edition
by Jason V. Barger**
All Rights Reserved. No part of this book may be used or reproduced in any manner whatsoever without written permission except in the case of brief quotations and references.

This book may be purchased for personal, educational, business, or sales promotional use. To obtain discounted bulk copies for your organization, please contact info@stepbackfromthebaggageclaim.com. For information please visit
www.StepBackFromTheBaggageClaim.com

Business Leader Edition - First Edition

ISBN: 978-0-615-35738-6

One Love Publishers

PRINTED IN THE UNITED STATES OF AMERICA
Cover Design: Adam Emery

BUSINESS LEADER EDITION

Change the World, Start at the Airport

by Jason V. Barger

One Love Publishers

"It's evidently contagious."
- The New York Times

The 4 Editions Of
Step Back from the Baggage Claim

Original Edition

Business Leader Edition

Healthcare Edition

Education Edition

Learn more at
www.StepBackFromTheBaggageClaim.com

This book is dedicated to my family and friends who walk with me every day and the countless individuals and organizations who have joined the *Step Back from the Baggage Claim* Movement. Thank you for choosing to put grateful, compassionate, creative, and servant-leadership ripples into action throughout our world!

Step Back from the Baggage Claim

CONTENTS

Foreword by Howard Behar	9
A Note From The Author	15
Boarding Pass (Introduction)	21
Step Back	29
You Are Now Free to Move About the Cabin	49
Seat 16 F: Ministry of Availability	71
Choose Your Own Adventure	89
Embrace *SkyMall*	111
Take Flight	129
FAQs About the Airport Journey . . .	156
Resources	162
21st Century Leadership	166
About the Author	167
Spread Your Book Around the World	168

Step Back from the Baggage Claim

Foreword by Howard Behar

I'm honored to be sharing my insights on how the spirit of ***Step Back from the Baggage Claim*** adds value to the development of a business leader or organization. In my 20 years with Starbucks, I realized that "It's Not About The Coffee". Our success, and the leadership that was at it's core, was about caring for people and inspiring each other to use our gifts to strengthen our mission.

It's my humble but firm belief that it is people - in the best of times and especially in the hardest of times - who will inspire you, sustain and grow your organization, and get you through. Even if financial resources are at hand to ease your business (whether from investors, banks, the government, good internal management, or family), it's not going to make any difference if everyone isn't committed, creative and purposeful about what you're doing. In the midst of the *obstacles, delays and cancellations* that you experience in business, the way your people respond to the challenges will determine your level of success.

Jason's message and the air travel metaphor are powerful anecdotes for leaders hoping to create a culture rooted in leadership, perspective, care, gratitude, intentionality, creativity and action. His story and passion reminds us how the small actions each day add up in the long run. That's how excellence is achieved - one small, thoughtful act at a time.

Here are a few of my targeted thoughts about the **Step Back from the Baggage Claim** leadership spirit:

- ***Step Back*** - In any group setting, from a team meeting to a department meeting to a companywide meeting, ask yourself, What do we stand for? What are we doing here? What do I need to contribute? So often the tendency is to rush right into the logistics of business that we forget to *Step Back* and ask the wider, deeper, more important questions that drive our efforts. Every business is trying to claim certain bags around that baggage claim, but the key is to be thoughtful about the system they create to claim them. Starting your work with a clear purpose and mission will tie everything you do together and provide a filter for efforts that don't fit with your vision. It takes discipline in the heat of the moment to *Step Back* and also requires dedicated time to *Step Back* and dream.

- ***Availability*** - Leadership is about caring for people. Caring is one of our most powerful resources, but often we don't reward and elevate leaders who master the ability to use it appropriately. For some reason, we seem to admire the stoic, stone-faced leader. However, the difference between an average manager and a great manager is that the latter understands that we can't hide our caring and still be genuine and effective. If we don't truly care about other people and have the guts to show it - even when things go badly - our humanity disappears. We must make time to be available for those we work with and work for. We have to remember that it's always about the people. We may be rewarded for the results we achieve in the organization, but we'll never know the results we might have achieved if we truly show we cared. Results without caring are empty results. They're just not sustainable. Being available and caring for those around us adds value in ways we can't always chart.

- ***An Ethic of Creativity*** - Dare to Dream. The ability to "dream of things that are not and ask, 'why not?'" is the most basic and primal of human motivations. What Starbucks has become and how it happened is a bigger dream than most of us could have imagined, and it is a dream that continues to come true for all of us who are part of the organization. It starts with a vision and core mission, but then moves into a commitment to daring to dream every day. That's where you have to create a culture where people and the values of your company come to life at work and just become second nature - as Jason says, "the way you move throughout the world".

Sales results and profits come from that commitment to ask 'why not?' and then act on passionate ideas.

- *Take Flight* - The purpose of all of this is to create an entity that you're proud of that produces positive results. My motto is, "Think like a person of action, and act like a person of thought." In some situations this means, "Feel. Think. Do." Other times it means "Feel. Do. Think." Most of the time, we want to think and then act, aim and then fire. If you're always fast to fire, you're likely to miss your shot - or get shot. If you're always waiting to fire, you're liable to miss an important opportunity. In our own leadership journey, as we learn who we are, we begin to know when to think, plan, and discuss and when to stop analyzing and take action. The principles of personal leadership - caring, listening for truth, being accountable - all require consistent action balanced with thought and feeling. You can't get results, you can't experience your potential, if you don't eventually take action. If you want to have an impact, if you aspire to make a difference, then you had better start doing it. Nothing is worse than wasting your life in the false comfort of inaction. Ideas and feelings eventually have to *Take Flight*!

Jason, and this book, aspire to make a difference - and are doing so as more and more people put this spirit into action in their organizations. He offers valuable reminders and simple principles that can guide the leadership actions you take in your own life and business. **Step Back from the Baggage Claim** is a call to each individual to bring a new spirit to the small moments of every day, and in doing so, change the world. I hope you'll join his movement and choose to *travel gracefully* throughout your business life.

-HOWARD BEHAR

President of Starbucks Coffee International, retired

Howard Behar joined Starbucks as a senior executive in 1989, when it had just twenty-eight stores. His positions have included executive vice president of sales and operations, president of Starbucks International, and president of Starbucks North America. He is a company advisor and served on the company's board of directors from 1996 to 2008. He lives in Seattle with his wife, Lynn. Learn more at www.howardbehar.com.

Step Back from the Baggage Claim

A Note From The Author

Step Back from the Baggage Claim was not written for the business world. It was written for our world. It was written to connect us to a more grateful, compassionate, thoughtful, and creative way to move throughout our world. It just so happens that many people have gravitated toward how this spirit also helps them navigate the obstacles, delays and cancellations in the business world. Much like the airport environment, our organizations are places that we move in and out of everyday - spaces where we cross paths with different people and different agendas and where we all share in the creation of the culture. So, the same question arises, what kind of culture do we want to create?

I remember sitting with Howard Behar, former President of Starbucks International, at the Greenleaf Center for Servant Leadership's International Conference. I was an Exhibitor at the Conference and the two of us sat outside the lecture hall for about 30 minutes, a long hallway basically to ourselves. He was normal, down to earth, and humble. I liked him very much.

Our conversation meandered about servant leadership, children, grandchildren, and yes, business. I learned very quickly from Howard (later confirmed in his speech and his book) that the success they had at Starbucks, when they grew from 28 domestic stores to hundreds of locations worldwide, was "not about the coffee". It was however, about invigorating people to bring their gifts to life to create an inspiring brand.

Similarly, his first words of wisdom to me about the ***Step Back from the Baggage Claim*** social movement were not focused on the bottom line, profitability, or clever marketing. Instead, his words were centered squarely on building relationships, telling an authentic story, and leading people toward a compelling vision. Then it just becomes a process of striving for excellence with each other every day. He and I were speaking the same language!

It got me thinking about that word 'process'. Defined simply by Dictionary.com as "a systematic series of actions directed to some end", not all processes are the same, but life is full of them. Right now my wife and I are in the process of managing a family of five. Our middle child, Benton, is in the process of learning how to form sentences. You may be in the process of dealing with a recent success or disappointing challenge. And irrefutably, your organization right now is in the process of leading the "series of actions" needed to reach the goals. We're never idle, we're always a part of a larger process.

My process for ***Step Back from the Baggage Claim*** grew out of years of pondering (often subconsciously) and with the vision of inspiring more grateful and compassionate actions in every day living. But, it only truly began when I made the first steps to bring the concept into reality - to put my own actions into motion. Since that pivotal point, it has been a dedicated, thoughtful, and courageous process of small choices about how to move forward with sharing this spirit.

As you begin the journey of this book I hope you make the choice to travel gracefully in your personal life, but I also invite you to consider how this spirit might impact your business life. If you're looking to create significant culture change that brings the spirit of this book to life within your organizational walls, then I hope you'll dive into an ongoing process of moving forward, as a team. This isn't a book revealing intricate business strategy, it is about how we choose to move with those we count on everyday to execute our strategy.

Imagine the next visioning or strategic planning initiative in your process as an individual, team or company. What if instead of racing to solutions, knee jerk reactions, status quo assumptions, or falling into the same uninspiring patterns that somehow become the norm, you commit to a thoughtful process of *Stepping Back from the Baggage Claim*?

Since the creation of the *Step Back from the Baggage Claim* movement, much of my time has been spent giving keynote speeches, leading workshops, and consulting with organizations regarding Culture Change, Servant Leadership, Innovation, and Leadership Development. The *Step Back* spirit has been resonating with businesses, non-profits, schools and universities, and churches. It has been abundantly clear to me that every organization benefits from taking time to not just think about "what" they do, but also to connect deeply to "why" and "how" they want to work in the world. In a racing world, we must find ways to:

- **Step Back** - *Step Back* from logistical thinking and begin with the question that must drive everything, "What is our mission and purpose for what we're doing?" Sounds simple, but it is a step that is often forgotten. When we are clear about our purpose and deeply rooted in "why" we do what we do, the "how" we choose to do it grows naturally out of the mission. The most common mistake in any kind of visioning process is not in being able to identify where you want to be at 'Point B', but it is when we don't take the time to clearly define what 'Point A' truly is. Don't race recklessly ahead, *Step Back,* find 'Point A'.

- **Be Still** - Commit time as individuals and as an organization to slow down and "Be Still". I guarantee it, you'll be better at what you do when you take time to reconnect, reflect, and refuel. It's counter-intuitive, but true.

- **Be Available** - Building relationships is the core of any successful entity. Call it networking. Call it team building. Or, just call it being human. When we drop our guard and allow ourselves to be *available* to those we sit next to on the airplanes, at the conference tables, or in the food courts, we open ourselves to authentic connections. It's a fact - when we connect with those we're "traveling with", we're better at what we do as a team. Make it a priority to put people in positions where they can break through impersonal modes of operation and build genuine connections.

- **Embrace Creativity** - Make it a priority in your business culture to allow space where ideas are free to wander, grow, perhaps die, but always lead to something else. When innovative questioning becomes a part of your DNA, mid-flight corrections won't just seem possible, it'll become just the way you fly.

- **Take Flight** - You can't remain in *Step Back* mode forever. If you do, paralysis by analysis will set in and forward progress will be stymied. The point of all of this is to *Step Back* to gain perspective in the midst of a racing world, but then to put actions into motion that make a difference. The gauge of any successful endeavor is whether clear action items lead you to *take flight*. The culture isn't changed merely by talking, it has to be followed up with action! What specific actions will lead to the culture you're hoping to create?

Good luck on your journey. That's what it is - a journey. It's not a 7 step program or a sprint to the first quick fix solution. It's a series of thoughtful, courageous and creative choices about how you want to move throughout your organization and your world.

Beyond this book, I'd love to add value to the process of strengthening the culture in your organization. I hope you'll join this movement and choose to share this spirit with others along your path. I'm passionate about connecting with great people to bring excellence, servant leadership, and creativity to life in the world.
Visit www.StepBackFromTheBaggageClaim.com to learn more.

Remember, leadership is about action. It is about standing up - showing a new vision for how we can move together. When we put loving and grateful actions into motion in the world, our world is changed! Need proof? Keep reading.

Travel Gracefully,

Jason Barger

Boarding Pass
(Introduction)

THE AIRPORT IS WHERE IT CAN BEGIN. I believe we can change the world. We can change the world because each one of us has the innate ability to expand our awareness, change our focus, and alter our daily interactions. The change I'm speaking of is not a naive, flip-of-the-switch, fairy-tale vision for the world, but rather, the profound ways in which small moments impact our lives every day. Solving the biggest problems in the world begins with the smallest of actions and an intentionally compassionate spirit. Every individual on this planet shares in the creation of today. Our everyday actions can bring about solutions right here, where we are right now.

According to the National Air Traffic Controllers Association, on any given day, more than 87,000 flights are in the skies over the United States. Even more impressive, the Transportation Security Administration (TSA) reports that 708,400,522 people were screened at security lines in U.S. airports during 2006. Every day, airports and airplanes are cities within cities, microcosms of much of American culture and behavior. Airports are where our adventures begin, places of our emotional goodbyes, spaces filled with frustration and chaos, and the public endpoint of our treks home.

The airport experience is the perfect metaphor for daily life in our world—so many different people going different directions with different agendas. Every leg of the journey offers obstacles. Nobody knows exactly how the journey is going to play out. There are moments of anticipation and excitement, disappointment and sadness. The stories behind most individuals are hidden, and each is unique. The skills required to navigate through the airport experience are the same skills needed to navigate every other phase of life. The ways we choose to live within the walls of the airport impact the ways we travel throughout the paths of our lives in the world.

We've all experienced the excitement of going on a new adventure, the frenzy at the ticketing counter, the anxiety at the security checkpoints, the frustration from a delay, the grumpy airline employee, the interesting fellow-traveler, and the wrestling match at the baggage claim. We've all witnessed the best and worst examples of humanity during our travels.

Every time I set foot in an airport my senses are heightened and my brain is on overdrive. Some of my most productive planning sessions, most pages read in one sitting, and most creative thoughts have arisen while seated in a rigid airplane seat or navigating a crowded terminal. I'm also fully aware of the imperfections of the airports, just as I'm fully aware of the imperfections of life. Airports and airplanes are places where our individual lives collide—giving us the opportunity to alter the world in some positive way for someone else by intentionally choosing to adjust our spirit in a few simple ways. We can provide significance to seemingly insignificant moments in someone's life.

Let me tell you about my journey. In 2004, I was leading 200 people to Tijuana, Mexico, to build homes for families living in poverty. In a matter of days, groups of fifteen high school students and adults would construct twenty-two-foot by eleven-foot houses for families that had been living in an eight-by-eight-foot makeshift lean-to in the dirt. That week twelve houses were built by our teams.

I remember landing in the San Diego airport to begin our adventure to Tijuana. I was sitting back and coordinating some of the trip logistics when our group approached the baggage claim. Our teams tried to assimilate into the already gathered mass of people. As the bags moved around the carousel, this glob of humanity struggled to claim their bags. In that moment, it was clear that the same patience, love, gratitude, generosity, and pace of life that we were going to need in Tijuana was needed around the baggage claim. I was reminded that the same spirit of compassion required to serve the families in Mexico is also needed in the small corners of our everyday lives. Not only do we have an opportunity to change the culture of the baggage-claim experience, we also have the opportunity to carry that loving spirit into other aspects of our lives. Perhaps the first step in making progress toward solving the biggest challenges in today's world is to truly practice generosity of spirit in the small moments of our lives.

Over the years, I have amassed a database of memories, notes of small details, quirky observations and experiences of human behavior in airports that reveal much about our world and culture in America today. I decided that bringing a compassionate spirit to airline travel has never been needed more than now, and perhaps that spirit could spill over to other areas of my life - family, friends, faith, and yes, business. To test this theory, I decided to go back to the airport—many airports—and to observe the way people interact with each other in their travels. I decided I should live in the airports and, at the same time, attempt to write a book that could benefit our world.

In 2008, I had recently stepped out of my job of ten years at First Community Church in Columbus, Ohio, as director of Camp Akita and leader of local and international service projects—ten unbelievable years filled with powerful relationships and work. I wouldn't change anything about that decade. In my final year, an internal sense called me to a new challenge. I was unsure of what was coming, but I knew I needed to be open and explore.

Leaving the comfort zone of a role that was going so well was a big step toward welcoming the next phase in my life. I made the conscious decision to take a leap of faith into the unknown with the hope of discovering more about myself, more about the challenges and opportunities available to me, and to discern what would be the next phase of my life. As I "stepped back from the baggage claim" in my own life to gain perspective, the next step in my adventure became clear: a creative endeavor to experience the unknown and learn more about our world. This book is the result.

So I began. I grabbed my legal pads of thoughts gathered throughout the years, my computer, and a small bag of clothes, and headed to the airport. I spent seven straight days in seven different cities. I flew 6,548 miles without stepping foot outside the airports, and soaked in roughly 10,000 minutes of observations at all four corners of the United States (Columbus, Boston, Miami, Chicago, Minneapolis, Seattle, and San Diego). Thank God for a lovingly supportive wife who cheers on my creative quest to live presently in the world!

I started in Columbus, Ohio. I wanted to reach all four corners of the United States in order to get a taste of the environment in different regions. I wanted to visit major airports, each representing cities that experience high traffic flow within the regions. I chose Boston because I had never been to that iconic East Coast city; Miami because it offers a highly diverse community of travelers; Chicago because it's Chicago; Minneapolis because it represents a dynamic Midwestern city; Seattle for its laid-back Pacific-Northwest charm; and San Diego because it is the portal to the southern California paradise. I allotted myself twenty dollars per day for expenses because of my unemployed status as well as my desire to experience each location very modestly. My only other rule was that I must constantly be in an airport or an airplane. I was there to observe, to learn, to be.

I wanted to write a book that could speak to anyone who has ever stepped inside an airport. I wanted to write a book that could connect with people of all backgrounds, all faith traditions, or no faith tradition at all. I wanted to write a book that could resonate with the business traveler, the soccer mom, the college student heading abroad, the flight-crew member who lives in this environment every day, TSA, the retired family member coming home, or the first-time traveler. I wanted to write a book that invites all of us to focus on what we have in common and suggests ways we can improve the environments where our lives cross. I wanted to write a book that would inspire others to bring a loving spirit to small actions, and then watch those actions permeate our world. I'm convinced that the lessons learned from our airport experiences can point us toward more fulfilling lives and toward a more compassionate world. If we really want to change the world, we need to start with small moments in our daily interactions. Since so many people travel by air daily, airports are the perfect locations to begin to affect change in our mobile world. This book uses air travel experiences as a metaphor for how each one of us can impact our world. If we want to change the world, let's start at the airport!

Let's also be clear at the outset. I'm not a moralist and I certainly do not wish to be mistaken for someone who thinks he has the answers to the world's questions. I'm simply a guy who wants to connect with people to make a positive change in our world. This is not a scientific study of human beings that will lay out answers to exactly why we act the way we do. It is a book that contains my observations of human behavior, of noticing the ways we bump into each other along life's journeys. What lies in the pages ahead are stories from my seven-day journey across the United States, my reflections on those experiences, as well as how they relate to other life experiences.

To the skeptic who may be asking himself in this very moment, "What's in this for me, and how will this make the slightest difference in my life," I say: Our happiness in life and life's purpose can be profoundly changed by our willingness to see the world differently. Seeking new perspectives, finding a new pace, expressing gratitude and compassion, and stretching our creativity can transform our small encounters into world changing habits. Living each moment of our lives with more awareness does positively impact all facets of our daily lives. But, we never fully understand that until we try.

Travel with me through the pages of this book and consider what our airport experiences can teach us about how we live our lives, how we move throughout our organizations, and what kind of leader we want to be in the world. Allow yourself the opportunity to slow down and accept the invitation to bring the spirit of this book to your daily life. Perhaps you'll choose to approach everyday travel excursions and business with a slightly different angle of vision and, maybe in the end, you too will believe we can change the world.

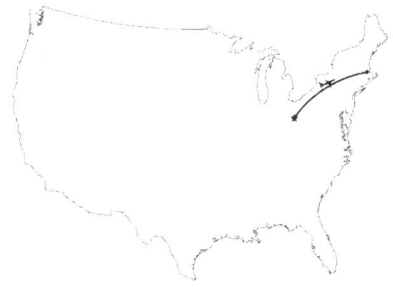

"Follow effective action with quiet reflection. From the quiet reflection will come effective action." - Peter Drucker

Step Back

THE BAGGAGE CLAIM SEEMED TO BE CALLING ME. I know it is backwards, but I began this random adventure in the Columbus airport at an empty baggage claim. From the beginning, this journey was not going to follow a conventional path. There was energy in the air and, like the calm before a storm, I was envisioning what soon would ensue at this very location.

We all know the scene. It is comical, yet frustrating. Our airplane lands at our destination city, and the hunt to claim what is ours begins. Hundreds (although it feels like thousands) of people scurry off the plane and begin their mad dash toward the baggage claim. Though everyone rushes, I can't remember the bags ever arriving at the baggage claim ahead of me. The sound of suit pants rubbing quickly back and forth and the whistling of fast-rolling wheels of carry-on luggage fill the air as the herd stampedes down the long terminal, hits the bottleneck at the escalator, and finally spills out into the baggage claim area.

The crowd gathers in anxious anticipation. Once that obnoxious buzzer goes off (Can't we come up with a better sound?), without fail, everyone scampers into place. Like Pavlov's dog, everyone reacts subconsciously to the buzzer and runs directly to the carousel. Within seconds, a human wall of hundreds (but now it seems like millions) is created, each person with their shins pressed against the cold metal carousel. Slowly, the bags begin emerging from the hidden baggage land, and the human wall shifts as each individual brick jockeys for "the best" position.

If you are one of the many who doesn't get out of the blocks quickly when the buzzer goes off, your 0.42-second lag-time costs you a spot at the carousel and an opportunity to see the bags. So you begin to bob and weave back and forth, jumping up and down to see over the tops of shoulders, dodging in and out of cracks, doing whatever you can to catch sight of your bags.

The ambitious percentage who arrive first at the carousel stand strong, protecting their spots, taking not even a second to let their eyes wander from the belt. Their knees are bent in an athletic stance, ready to pounce on the first bag that dares to look even slightly similar to their own. They do not budge an inch until they get *their* bags from the spot *they* earned.

Meanwhile, the frail older woman with the cute pink flowered hat and dangling earrings is trying to wade through the chaos. She is having a hard time as it is, carefully navigating through the thick crowds without losing her balance, obviously flustered by the frantic pace of the scene. Through one of the few cracks in the "human wall of entitlement," she spots her beat-up olive-green suitcase, circa 1963. With a couple of "excuse me's" and another "I'm sorry," she gets the wall to part just long enough so she can grasp her bag's passing handle.

She tugs with all of her might, and the bag slowly wiggles off of the belt, crashing into the bags on either side, and bouncing off the human wall. As she struggles to gain control of the bag, barely lifting it from the passing belt onto solid ground, the opening in the human wall reverts to a fortress.

Every time I'm at the baggage claim I search for the best observation post. The same cast of characters always shows up. I watch the madness, frustration, and inefficiency of each person trying to locate their bags, and I can't help but think there could be a better way to experience the baggage claim. I daydream and imagine myself moving to the center of the mob and yelling out to the crowd:

Hey, everyone . . . I've got a great idea . . . from now on, how about (whenever we come to a baggage claim) we take three steps back from the conveyer belt so that everyone can see. Once you see your bag coming toward you, go ahead and step toward the belt to retrieve your bag. And oh, by the way, when we see someone who needs help lifting their bag from the belt . . . how about if we help them! (This last part is delivered with a slightly humorous tone.)

In this daydream, everyone is startled and confused as my voice jolts them from the baggage claim tug-o-war, but the look on their faces confirms that this is a good idea, and some actually even begin to laugh. I scan the eyes of those scrunched up to the conveyer belt; it is as if a lightbulb went off in the collective consciousness of the group, and everyone thinks, "Oh yeah . . . of course." I wonder: Could this dream become reality? Could we actually change our routine and, subsequently, the spirit at the baggage claim?

Just imagine what the experience at the baggage claim would be like if everyone took those three steps back so everyone could see, and if everyone actually helped those around them with their bags. Not only would the spirit and environment around the conveyer belt be more positive for all, but it also would be a more efficient way for everyone to get their bags as quickly as possible. Imagine if *stepping back at the baggage claim* became the norm; imagine how that inclusive spirit could impact the underlying tone of complaining that permeates other aspects of the airport. A place commonly filled with chaos, negativity, and frustration would be changed because of the thoughtful awareness of many. Then, imagine what that same spirit could mean for the world if we carried it into other areas of our lives as well.

I've watched this happen so many times (not the daydream—the baggage claim tug-o-war) and it still is comical. I've watched business travelers, mothers with young children and college students back from an adventure abroad all contribute to the silliness of the human wall. Witnessing this scene in Columbus, Boston, Miami, Chicago, Minneapolis, Seattle, and San Diego for seven straight days was quite revealing.

I don't believe everyone who crowds the conveyer belt is merely a selfish person who doesn't recognize the needs of others. I choose to believe that, in most cases, the mayhem at the conveyer belt occurs because we just aren't thinking about what we're doing. My guess is that the very same person who is aggressively jockeying at the conveyer belt would not only benefit from stepping back from the baggage conveyor belt, but could use a step back in other areas of their life as well. Taking a step back from the conveyor belt is a conscious decision to gain new perspective, include others and see the interests of others as well as your own.

I could certainly launch into a commentary right now and cite all kinds of sources that suggest how greedy we Americans are and how our "survival of the fittest" mentality has bred us to turn even the simple task of claiming our bags into a competition. I could jump to the conclusion that in the midst of our greed, we are only concerned about what we think we are entitled to and, in the end, not interested in those around us. I could go down those roads, but I'm choosing to believe we simply aren't thinking about it. As in many other areas of our lives, we are simply on autopilot and fall into line the way the person in front of us does without giving it much thought. Somewhere back in our history, crowding the baggage conveyor belt became the norm for how we gather our bags. No better system or consciousness was given to the act so we just followed the example of the person before us. Now it is time to do it differently.

The reason I choose to believe we simply aren't thinking about a better way to approach the baggage claim experience is because I'm continually amazed with all the people around me who do care about others. They are everyday people, just like you and me, who spend considerable amounts of time thinking about how to care for those around them. They are people focused on living their lives with meaning, caring for their family members, and trying to smile at the stranger in the grocery store. My experience is that people are basically good and want to be kind to others; that, deep down, we all have a yearning to connect and care for something beyond ourselves. We all have lapses and moments of autopilot behavior that may cause us to stray from our core values without awareness of it. It is time to step back from the baggage claim and reexamine how our actions can reflect those core values.

Why write a book built around illustrations as arbitrary as picking up your luggage from the baggage claim? Our lives are a string of baggage-claim moments—opportunities to change our world through new awareness! Our organizations can often feel like one overcrowded baggage claim - everyone trying to claim what they think is theirs. We all are trying to claim certain bags around the metaphorical baggage claim of life. We're trying to claim happiness, money, security, love, friendship, recognition, expectations, and in many cases, just stuff we think we need. If we become aware of the lessons to be learned in those baggage-claim moments, we can begin to articulate what they mean for other areas of our lives. If we commit to stepping back at the baggage claim, then perhaps we can begin to acknowledge the other areas of our lives that are in need of a "step back." Any time we find ourselves getting so close to something that our view of the bigger picture becomes distorted, it's time to step back.

This happens in our personal lives and our business lives - momentary lapses around that crowded baggage claim that cause us to get caught up in the madness and often lose sight of our ultimate purpose. James Collins and Jerry Porras, in their highly acclaimed business book *Built To Last*, share words from a speech given by David Packard to his staff at Hewlett-Packard (HP) during a critical time in its existence.

> "I want to discuss *why* (emphasis his) a company exists in the first place. In other words, why are we here? I think many people assume, wrongly, that a company exists simply to make money. While this is an important result of a company's existence, we have to go deeper and find the real reasons for our being. As we investigate this, we inevitably come to the conclusion that a group of people get together and exist as an institution that we call a company so that they are able to accomplish something collectively that they could not accomplish separately - they make a contribution to society, a phrase which sounds trite but is fundamental."

How easy it is to stand around the hustling baggage claims of our organizations, losing sight of our core mission, and just diving into 'getting things done'. In doing so, we find ourselves chasing tangents, wasting efforts, developing bad habits, and forgetting our ultimate purpose. It's in those moments that it's time to *step back* and think about how we want to move throughout the world.

I have no doubt that how we act at the baggage claim is an indicator of how we may approach other aspects of life. Changing small interactions in our lives can transfer into the larger areas of our lives! Culture change begins with one small act at a time.

Remember President Ronald Reagan challenging the Soviets in his famous 1987 speech beside the Berlin Wall in Germany:

> Today I say: As long as the gate is closed, as long as this scar of a wall is permitted to stand, it is not the German question alone that remains open, but the question of freedom for all mankind. . . .
>
> Mr. Gorbachev, TEAR DOWN THIS WALL!

When I was in the eighth grade and my family stood beside the Berlin Wall, I didn't fully comprehend what we were doing. We were at the wall, rocks in hand on a chilly December day, and my family helped to tear down that wall. People lined the wall swinging sledge hammers and sending chunks of concrete flying around the historic Brandenburg Gate. The wall could have been taken down in a much more efficient manner by professionals, but the image of commoners from around the globe chipping away at oppression sent a message that reverberated around the world. I'm so fortunate my parents saw the value in that symbolism and, despite my adolescent short-sightedness, stood with me at the wall. They allowed me to experience the celebration of a new way of living in the world. They also sent a loud and clear message: Walls are not the answer to the problems in our lives.

With much less at stake, certainly with less fanfare, and definitely not a literal comparison to the Berlin Wall, I say: Let's tear down the human wall at the baggage claim and, with each flight, make a statement about how we choose to live together. Let's declare a new way to approach the baggage claim—a new spirit for the small moments in our lives. Let's step back at the baggage claim and see what awareness the experience of stepping back could bring to other spaces in our lives. Let's TEAR DOWN THIS HUMAN WALL!

Back-to-School Night

We often get too close to the conveyer belt in other areas of our lives and need to step back from the baggage claim. My wife Amy has been a special education teacher for eight years. Recently she recalled a scene from one of her back-to-school nights—when parents attend an orientation with their children's teachers. As the evening was coming to an end, all of the teachers lined up in the hallways, and the parents were invited to hang around to ask any specific questions regarding their particular child.

This night, Amy happened to be standing in the hall right next to one of the specialists who was filling in for a sick teacher and answering parents' questions. In the brief ten-minute post-orientation barrage of questions in the hallway, Amy witnessed nearly a dozen sets of parents approach this teacher with one critical question, "What does our child need to do in kindergarten, first or second grade in order to be chosen for the gifted program that begins in third grade?"

That was their burning question! Not one set of parents asked anything specific about their child's current learning experience in the classroom or provided the teacher with insight about their child's behavior at home. Not one set of parents had additional questions about the curriculum presentation they had heard earlier or further questions about teaching styles. Not one question dealt with their child's present learning experience. Every set of parents was focused on one thing— eventually getting their kid into the exclusive gifted program. Each of those parents was overlooking the small, but critical, events in the life of their child at the present moment.

I know it is natural for parents to desire affirmations that their child is bright. Parents who are active and committed to providing the best educational opportunities for their kids are to be applauded. However, this is a real-life example of people getting stuck on autopilot, oblivious to the current situation, and fixated on the reward that has yet to come down the conveyer belt. Those parents seemed to be hovering too close to the conveyer belt, so anxious about the future that their view of the big picture in life was being distorted. They were in need of a giant step backwards to gain perspective.

When I heard that story, I couldn't help thinking that an opportunity was lost for those parents. This was their great opportunity to step back from the madness of the crowd, from expectations, from future aspirations, from labels such as "gifted," and celebrate their child as he or she is—now. In our high-octane determination to give our kids the best, are we skipping the all-important step of appreciating their current stage of development so they are prepared and confident enough to move forward into the future? Are we getting ahead of ourselves so much that a child may receive the mixed message that the gifted program in the future is more important than what he learns or how he or she feels today? STEP BACK! Purposefully create some space to gain perspective on what is most important at this exact moment. It's so easy in our businesses to get obsessive about our "Long Range Plans" that we forget to execute our business with excellence today. Instead of worrying excessively about the future, celebrate now and learn something today that will lead you into the future. Let's be people who are able to step back from the madness of the crowd and claim a new angle of vision.

Haiti

I had to take a giant step back. In 1999, I visited my cousin Robert who was serving with the Peace Corps in Haiti. This came shortly after I had begun my work at the church. My initial role was assisting the talented Rev. John Ross with our high-school students, leading our college staff at our idyllic Camp Akita in the Hocking Hills of southern Ohio, and bringing leadership to the development of service projects locally and internationally. I quickly gravitated toward serving and developing our mission efforts. So, I jumped at the opportunity to visit a country such as Haiti and see the need firsthand.

I stayed with Robert and his host family in the rural village of Cayes Jacmel. It took us nearly three hours in the back of a gutted, old school bus packed with about sixty-five people to get from the capital of Port-Au-Prince to Cayes Jacmel. Staying in the same cramped position on a rough three-hour bus ride brings stark, contrasting, awareness to our complaints about the crowded airplanes in which we travel. Haiti has earned its spot near the top of the list of struggling countries in the world, and witnessing the depleted resources of the countryside confirmed that reality for me. Although the hillsides were trashed and burned, the beauty of the people and the ways they cared for my cousin despite such meager resources was a powerful experience. Besides completing his various Peace Corps-related duties, we spent the balance of the week enjoying the culture and village community with his new friends.

My "step back" moment came on one of my last mornings in Cayes Jacmel. The term "hot as Haiti" is not just a saying. We arose with the sun because the day was sweltering by mid-morning. Our normal routine was to wake up at dawn, head down to the makeshift basketball court my cousin had taken great pride in restoring, play some games with the locals before it was unbearably hot, pour buckets of water over our sweaty bodies, and return to his host family's house by early morning for breakfast.

I had just finished changing out of my basketball clothes and gotten dressed for the day when I noticed a Haitian man standing in the doorway of the room. In the worst Creole he had ever heard, I said "bonswa" and welcomed him into the room. He was holding the cutest baby boy I had seen (my own children came some years later!). He handed me the child and I sat on the edge of the bed making the baby laugh, soaking in the chance to snuggle with such an adorable little fellah. The father was speaking to me while I played with the boy, but he didn't quite understand that my Creole was infantile at best.

My cousin entered the room after about ten minutes of play time and interrupted the man's speaking.

"J, do you know what the man is saying?" Robert asked. I flashed him my "I-speak-infantile-Creole" look.

"He is asking you to take his baby back to the United States with you."

I looked into the man's eyes and allowed several seconds for this to sink in.

"He says that he feels you would take good care of him and he knows his son will have a much better life in the States," my cousin continued, as my thoughts swirled.

My body was shocked still. My mind, heart, and world took a giant step back. It wasn't as if I couldn't imagine someone asking such a thing or wanting the very best for his child, but it was the look in his eyes that I'll never forget. The sincerity, the deep abiding love, desire for a better world for his son, and the willingness to make such a profound sacrifice, were piercing. My "step back" was not just perspective-altering, but a moment filled with crippling sadness, overwhelming gratitude, profound helplessness, and a great desire to serve.

My mind searched for solutions, and my heart raced as I questioned whether I could indeed take his son. At the age of twenty-three, was I ready to raise a son? I was overwhelmed by my imagined logistics of getting a Haitian baby back into the United States. I had no immediate solution to his request. In that moment, I wasn't able to help that man or his son other than to express genuine love for them in those few minutes. I'll never forget the look in the father's eyes. His look confirmed my deep desire to serve those in need and to live in the world with gratitude.

I recalled that look later as we developed our *Streets Mission Project* to serve the homeless in Columbus, and again as we built 120 houses in Mexico and 5 in the Dominican Republic for families living in the dirt. That Haitian man has no idea that the look in his eyes that day, and the "step back" it caused, has had a ripple effect throughout my life. The look I saw in his eyes is still with me today.

Stepping Back from the Baggage Claim is about gaining perspective, seeing the world from a different angle of vision. It is about creating space and allowing for something greater to emerge. My aunt has a quote from writer Anais Nin on her kitchen wall that I look at every time I'm at her house. It says, "We don't see things as they are, we see them as *we* are." We tend to stand around the conveyer belts of our lives thinking about what we have to do, and how we are going to get there—fixated on how to quickly claim what we wish to claim as ours. We aren't intentionally losing our focus on reality or ignoring the many other people standing at that very same conveyer belt. We've just slipped into our default setting of "how *we* are" and that clouds our inclusive vision. In a global economy, clouded vision of "how *we* are" can lead us to forget the true needs of the diverse population around that baggage claim.

If we can understand and accept that we see the world through the lens of who we are and where we are, then it is even more important to step back to adjust our perspective of reality. In the process of stepping back we allow time, space, and the opportunity to see things with fresh eyes. My hope is that when we step back to examine our lives and our organizations, we try to live in the present moment and to appreciate all the others who also stand at the conveyer belt.

Frances Hesselbein, the person that management guru Peter Drucker once suggested was the greatest leader in the country (during her time as National Executive Director of the Girl Scouts), once said,

> Peter Senge told us; 'Mission instills passion and patience for the long journey.' If we can summon both the passion to pursue that journey and the patience to stop for travelers we meet along the way, our organizations will be well served indeed.

Stepping Back from the Baggage Claim is really more about spreading out—creating important space for all. In that process of stepping back and connecting to our Mission we authentically serve those around us. We must not only allow ourselves to stop for the travelers around us but, even more significantly, we must allow our eyes to see the inherent and irreplaceable value of each person who also stands around the conveyer belt. We need to step back, create space, see with new eyes, and claim the more inclusive life. Leadership is about taking a stand - showing a new vision for how we can move together.

Questions For Your Journey . . .
Stepping Back in Your Organization

Stepping back from the baggage claim in life begins with identifying the areas where we may be too close to the conveyer belt. Is there a situation at work where your intense focus on a goal, a strenuous relationship, or a fast-moving project has caused you to lose sight of the big picture? Are there small moments when things seem out of control—a meeting that seems to be getting off track, a never-ending 'to do list', a negative comment from your boss, or a frustrating e-mail? **Stepping back** *is about providing space, allowing for a new angle of vision, and recognizing the needs of others. It is about claiming a new spirit for how we choose to operate in the crowded spaces of our organizations. In a racing world with high expectations, we cannot forget to stop every once in awhile and reconnect to our Mission and Vision. The first phase of moving forward in those hectic moments begins with the thoughtful process associated with stepping back.*

- *Why am I doing the work that stands before me?*
- *What area of my work could use a "step back" to gain perspective?*
- *Is my team rooted on Mission and Purpose?*
- *How can my team be more efficient claiming our bags?*
- *In what way(s) will I step back from the baggage claim today?*

Step Back
Gain Perspective and Create Space for Others

Notes

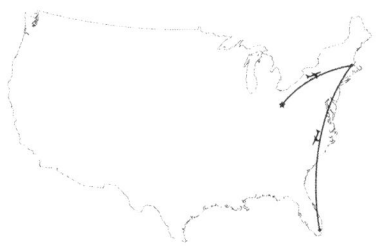

"One's action ought to come out of an achieved stillness: not to be mere rushing on." - D. H. Lawrence

You Are Now Free to Move About the Cabin

SHE WAS INTRIGUING. I made my way down the aisle of the airplane and located my seat by the window. She was seated in the aisle seat of my row, and the middle seat remained empty. This was the first flight (Columbus to Boston) of my seven-day adventure in seven different airports and all four corners of the United States. As I took my seat, her nose was buried in a folder full of documents. She appeared to be in her late-forties to early-fifties, and she barely acknowledged me when I made my way past her to the window spot. I didn't mind, she was concentrating.

The heading on her folder read "Oxfam." This immediately piqued my interest due to my appreciation for the nonprofit sector and organizations dedicated to serving the world. Oxfam is an international organization committed to finding solutions to poverty and social injustice. It operates in over 100 countries and, to my knowledge, does its job well; Charity Navigator, the leader in charity evaluation, gives them a four star rating.

My seat-mate was extremely focused and seemed detail-oriented as she combed each line of the pile of documents she was holding. I noticed she was reading over a job description for what appeared to be a position as Regional Director with Oxfam America, which serves the Gulf Coast region. As she thumbed back and forth between the job description, her resume, a reference list, and personal notes, it was clear she was preparing for an interview at Oxfam's Boston headquarters. I could feel the intensity, anxiety, and focus radiating from her.

Nearly half-way through the flight, someone in the row behind us kicked our seats a few times. Before I could turn my head around to see who it was, the woman next to me whipped her head around and said in a harsh tone, "Would you PLEASE stop that!"

The woman in the row behind us quickly and sincerely replied, "I'm sorry, he's only sixteen months old . . . I'm trying to contain him."

My seat-mate didn't even respond. She just went right back to her papers. She wasn't willing to slow down. She was in a hurry.

In that moment I wished the people at Oxfam, who would soon be interviewing her in Boston, could have witnessed this encounter. Not because I wished her bad luck or because I'm surprised by such behavior (we all have our chippy moments), but because that small event may have been the single best indicator of how she might perform on the job. Start small. If we can't even deal in a caring manner with a sixteen-month-old kicking our airplane seat, how are we going to provide aid and care to the entire Hurricane Katrina-ravaged Gulf Coast?

I know it is not fair to judge a person solely on one random encounter and an obviously stressful moment. Believe me, I don't want my career abilities to be judged based on a snippy comment I made because someone at Dunkin' Donuts spilled coffee on my computer bag. Perhaps my seat-mate was the most qualified candidate and would be key to leading the rebuilding efforts in Louisiana and beyond.

My point is this: only when we begin to handle the small events of our lives well can we begin to address the bigger challenges. If someone truly hopes to improve the lives of people in the world (as interest in the Oxfam position certainly would suggest), then that person has to start by bringing the same compassion, empathy, and loving spirit to those we bump into every day. Leadership—true authentic leadership that connects rather than divides—

demands this type of spirit daily. A leader of a country, organization, company, division, team, council, family or just that little voice within that leads each individual must represent the very best of his or her mission and values. A leader must treat the doorman well, express gratitude to the servers in a restaurant, and appreciate his or her administrative assistants. Nobody is perfect in every moment, but there is an infectious spirit and energy that comes from small, yet caring, encounters. World-changing leadership begins at this level—the airport level—and then moves people passionately into larger arenas with the potential for more significant change.

We all know the speech that the flight attendant shares with us before every airplane takes off. They give direction to those traveling with children: In case of an emergency, first put on your own oxygen mask, then the child's. That image is a powerful one for our lives. Make sure to take the time to meet your own health needs so you then are able to meet the needs of others. In the airplane emergency, our own health need is about the oxygen. It isn't only about getting off the plane or accomplishing your next task—yet. It is first about inhaling enough oxygen continuously so you are capable of taking the next step. When we are in a hurry, even if our intentions are good, we can't forget to slow down and breathe so we can also recognize the needs of those around us. It is possible to move quickly through life without hurrying.

As our plane descended into Boston, I reflected on my first flight and hurried pace of our lives. I thought about the lofty expectations and intense pressures that exist in our careers that can often feel like heavy baggage we're lugging around. I wanted to give the woman in my row the benefit of the doubt and chalk her reaction up as a moment where her life was just speeding too quickly. Once the front wheels of the aircraft touched the runway, Southwest Airlines was on my mind. Southwest Airlines had cleverly modified the common airline phrase "You are now free to move about the cabin" to "You are now free to move about the country" as its slogan. The Southwest Airlines' bell, or "ding," is also a part of that brand—accompanying the slogan every time it's used. The ding upon arrival at your destination is the universal signal to toss the seatbelt aside and rise out of your seat.

Our small plane of about forty-five people lands at Boston's Logan International Airport. We're all accustomed to the routine: The ding sounds and, just as predictably as at the baggage claim, everyone immediately begins scurrying. I'm seated in row 6 of this fifteen-row plane—the perfect spot from which to watch the rise of passengers behind me and the general hustle as the plane door opens in the front.

Everyone around me quickly grabs their loose items, and nearly 80 percent of the plane is already standing. It feels weird, and is certainly not the norm, to sit still. The most comical sight is the people who quickly dash down the aisle at the sound of the ding to gain a row or two. From two rows behind me (row 8), a man in a sharp-looking business suit darts at the sound of the ding and makes it "all the way to row 5" by the time the woman in the aisle seat of row 5 stands to collect her bags. Even in the victory of gaining three rows, he still has to wait.

The airplane's door does not open immediately. We all know that, don't we? The ding goes off giving us the signal it is safe to get out of our seats and begin gathering our belongings—but it hardly means that it is time to disembark. So there we sit or (80 percent) stand. Now everyone is crammed in an even more awkward position than when we were neatly seated in our assigned seats—yet the rush is on. So, we sit, stand, check our cell phones, talk about how much of a hurry we are in, and engage in uncomfortable small talk with the person whose head is now directly below our armpit.

The funniest thing about this scene is that, once the airplane door does finally open, we still aren't finished waiting. Of the estimated forty-five passengers on board this particular flight, twenty of us stepped outside the airplane and onto the tarmac to wait for our carry-on bags that had been "stowed" underneath the plane (when else do we use the word "stow" in normal conversation?). And, of course, standing in that group of twenty people, for at least another eight minutes, was the guy who made the highly strategic dash from row 8 to row 5 at the sound of the ding. And . . . twenty minutes later, I see many familiar faces from the flight waiting in line at the first Starbucks they can find in the airport. But, they're still in a hurry.

Why are we in such a hurry? Are we *actually* in such a hurry? Does darting about quickly make us feel as though we are more important than someone else? Is it okay to assume that we are in more of a hurry than the person next to us on the plane or—better yet—the majority of the others on the plane? Is our schedule more important or too valuable to just sit patiently, relax, and move when it is our turn to move? We all learned the whole "taking turns" principle as a young child. My son Will had a fairly extensive grasp of the concept of taking turns at the age of three.

This would be another opportunity to spout a litany of illustrations (of which we all are fully aware by now) regarding the current pace of our culture. I could cite statistics about the number of hours we are working, the number of households with two working parents, the technologically connected world of which we all are a part, etc. But, I don't want to do that. We are aware of those things and know life in the twenty-first century will continue to challenge us in new and unique ways.

What I am suggesting is that slowing ourselves down will not just literally slow things down, but will allow us to live more fully. Admittedly, I am someone who loves a fast pace and often operates in a "let's work hard and get things done" mentality. I cannot operate at a standstill for too long before I get antsy to create and connect. I know these things about myself. However, I also know my work is better, I'm a better teammate, I'm a better friend, I'm a better husband, I'm a better father, and I'm a better contributor to the world when I slow down and allow myself to live fully in each moment. Slowing down doesn't mean stopping. Slowing down means pressing the brakes from time to time — long enough to see the view from the window, or the person on the side of the road. It means actually listening clearly to the person talking to us in the front seat. Slowing down is looking someone in the eyes. The agenda of the world is bigger than our personal agenda; there is more to see and contribute than just exiting the airplane door first. Perhaps slowing down at the sound of the ding would serve us in other areas of our lives as well. If we are able to discipline ourselves to see the value of slowing down at the ding on the airplane then maybe we will be able to transfer that same spirit into other moments in life. Then, when we need it most during a hurried time in life, we'll be prepared to thoughtfully slow down rather than recklessly race past those on our path.

Be Still

In his book, *The Space Between the Notes,* Dr. Richard Wing's depiction of the Bible story from Mark 4:35–42, in which Jesus calms the storm on the Sea of Galilee, stays with me to this day. If you're not religiously orientated (it's okay), hang with me, the point is applicable!

For years, whenever this story was referenced, I pictured how it went. There was Jesus with the disciples out in a boat when a storm came up quickly. Jesus was kicking back for a nap in the back of the boat while the waves got higher and higher. With each crashing wave the disciples grew more and more worried about their fate. Finally they dashed to the back of the boat to wake Jesus. He walked to the front of the boat and yelled out, "Quiet! Be still!" and the waves slowly subsided.

The story made sense in a Biblical Savior / Jedi Knight / Prophet kind of way. As usual, Jesus rushed to the scene and showed his all-encompassing power over even the waves of the ocean. I enjoyed the story, but I'm not sure it fully resonated with me until Wing invited me to see it from a different angle.

"When the words 'peace, be still' are spoken, they are addressed to persons, not the weather," Wing wrote. All of a sudden the story reverberated with me more deeply. In our desire to focus only on Jesus as the superhero, we forget to listen to the message behind the actions. Perhaps Wing was right. Maybe Jesus really wasn't speaking to the waves. Maybe he was talking directly to the world. Maybe he wanted that image to teach us that no matter how big or small the waves of life get, take time to "Quiet! Be still!" Slow down.

I know that in the few storms that have appeared in my privileged life, stepping back, creating space, allowing stillness, and having faith that the waves would subside has made a huge difference. As I've made the move into larger leadership positions around larger baggage claims in my life, the practice of quieting my outer world in order to listen to my inner voice has been vital. Robert K. Greenleaf, in his 1977 perspective-altering book *Servant Leadership,* reminded us that if individuals are going to bring about change in the world or in their organizations, it has to start from the center.

Greenleaf wrote, "If a flaw in the world is to be remedied, to the servant the process of change starts in here, in the servant, not out there." He reminded us that if we want to change the world it has to begin with our individual efforts. It must begin with our internal decision to move thoughtfully in our external world.

Could our commitment to slow down at the sound of the ding carry over into other important areas of our lives? If "practice makes perfect," could the awareness and intention in these smaller moments prepare us for bigger challenges to come?

The over-sixty-year mission at Camp Akita in southern Ohio focuses on providing a dynamic environment in which kids of all ages are welcomed in a fun, nonthreatening way. Akita is nearly 1,300 beautiful acres—almost all of it untouched wilderness. The small percentage of the grounds used for the camp include sixteen open-air cabins sitting on the sloped hillside, two athletic fields, a high-ropes course, and a modern lodge and dining hall overlooking the focal point of the camp: the lake. Trees surround the center of camp and contribute to the feeling that when you come to Akita, you have escaped away to a separate, special world.

As an Akita staffer for thirteen years and the camp director for four years, I tried my best to carry out the mission. Kids from all faith traditions (or no faith tradition) are welcomed and celebrated. Kids can spot a phony from a mile away, and the last thing they want is for someone to tell them what to believe (I don't want that either). It was our privilege, as dedicated staff at Camp Akita, to create a uniquely loving and open environment where people are embraced exactly where they are in their lives and allowed the freedom and respect to search *their* questions about what matters most to *them*.

Activity fills the week: high-ropes courses, huge soap slides down a hillside, aqua trampolines on the lake, basketball games, and bizarrely clever skits put on by a phenomenal college staff. On the next-to-last night, the campers follow one of the many hiking trails into the woods, wind through the forest, and make their way up the steepest hill in all the campgrounds. The last stretch of path up the hill feels like a peaceful tunnel through arching tree limbs . . . until you come out of the path into a wide open meadow on the top of the hill. The grassy overlook is at the highest point in the area and is surrounded by trees.

In the spirit of the same stillness experienced that day on the Sea of Galilee, the camp community of over 200 spreads out over the entire hillside and begins a twenty-minute period of silence—not exactly the kind of event that you would expect to be appealing to kids, but you'd be amazed how sacred that time becomes as kids move into different stages in their lives. In today's wonderful world of twitter, Ipods, Facebook, and video games, it is increasingly important that we disconnect technologically, even if only briefly, and to personally connect to something deeper. Some of the kids even admit that this is the only time during the entire year when they sit still for twenty minutes without any agenda or distractions. They have time to think about who they are and who they want to be.

There is no possible way to measure the impact these twenty-minute sessions have on the lives of the people on that hill. I can't point specifically to a fight among adolescent friends that was avoided, to a more loving and compassionate way they chose to treat their parents upon returning home or, even more dramatically, the harm that was not done to themselves or others by a kid feeling useless and hopeless in life. I can't put up a graph that pinpoints the success of these "be still" moments, but I can tell you that I've seen it in the eyes of those on that hill; I've also witnessed it in my own life. Slowing down, sitting still on that gorgeous hilltop as the sun crosses behind the treeline, and taking the time to think about who I wanted to be in this world has helped shape who I am today.

We don't always have to jump right out of our seats at the sound of each ding. The discipline of stillness, of slowing down, could become the norm on airplanes. Then, that discipline could stay with us into the other important work we have to do in the world.

Howard Behar, during the process of leading Starbucks' expansion from twenty-eight stores to hundreds of stores around the globe, spoke to the importance of finding stillness and silence.

"You'll be amazed at the power of silence. Pay attention to how people fill it. What questions, worries, and issues do they fill it with? Their insecurity? Their confusion? A problem that has been weighing on their mind? Or see what happens when you put a topic on the table and simply ask, 'How do you feel about that?' Sometimes the hardest thing to do is listen when nothing is being said. Many times people want to fill that space. Keep your ears open, your eyes open, and your mouth not flapping. Give it time. Let the silence fill itself. It may mean thirty seconds. It may mean a minute. It may be five minutes. But it will come. You get to the bottom of a lot of problems quickly by trusting the silence to reveal the heart of things."

Finding moments of stillness in a racing world allows us to perform our best in the moments we have. We usually cannot quantify the impact our still moments have on the excellence of our individual work or the contributions they make to our organizational culture - but they do matter. They allow us to catch our breath, connect back to our Mission and Purpose, and refuel us to move forward. Perhaps practicing stillness at the ding will allow us to use our energy to deal with the next larger challenge that may appear only minutes down the road.

Four Breaths

In 1924, George Mallory and Andrew Irvine set out to climb Mount Everest. They disappeared near the summit and, ever since, explorers from around the globe have been trying to figure out what happened to them. A few years back, I had the pleasure of meeting Andy Politz. Politz was a member of the Mallory and Irvine Research Expedition. He was present when Mallory's body was found in May of 1999. The discovery resulted in a worldwide stir, two TV documentaries and numerous articles. In total, Politz participated on seven Everest Expeditions. He speaks to diverse groups about his experience and the lessons he learned along the way.

He detailed the effort it took to accomplish even the smallest task when people reached a certain altitude on Everest because of the lack of oxygen. When you climb high enough, you have to take four breaths for every action you want to perform. You can't get enough oxygen with just one breath, so you have to take four deep breaths . . . and then move. He painted the picture of waking up in his tent around 3 a.m. because it was going to take a long time to prepare for climbing by dawn. Four breaths, sit up. Four breaths, light the lantern. Four breaths, put a shoe on. Four breaths, put the other shoe on. That would continue until they had everything packed up and were ready to begin climbing. And then, of course, four breaths were required to take one step. Four breaths, take another step. The pace, dedication, patience and symbolism within that image is powerful.

In the first couple of weeks after my mom was diagnosed with breast cancer in 2007, the image of four breaths on Everest came alive to me. I talked with her about the "four breaths" during her first chemotherapy treatment. None of us knew what the journey ahead was going to be like; in an instant, life had switched to a different pace. We had no choice but to embrace the slower pace. Cancer treatment is a journey of sequences of taking four deep breaths and then placing one foot in front of the other. From day one, my mom was a glowing example of that determined pace. I'm continually impressed by her strength, optimism, and focus on what's important. This health crisis was a reminder to our family that the ding of the bell actually means slow down, breathe deeply, and then take a step.

Usually, it isn't hard to spot someone operating at a slower pace than the normal American sprint. However, knowing, understanding, and appreciating why they are operating at that speed is a whole different story. We often are unaware of the heavy baggage people are carrying around with them every day.

A few years back, I stepped foot into a particular discount grocery store for the first time. It had opened in our area roughly a year earlier and was all the rage for the bargain hunters. The buzz was that it was the perfect spot for families trying to save some money on their monthly food costs. My wife shopped there a couple of times, but I hadn't until this day. I was out running errands in the area when I spotted the store and got excited about giving it a try. I had to grab just a couple of items, so I eagerly moved inside.

From my first step beyond their front door, I knew this was going to be different. I couldn't even determine which direction was the entrance and which was the exit. After a quick attempt to orient myself, I waded my way into the crowded store.

Instantly I had a better understanding of why they were able to cut costs. They obviously saved time and money in at least three key areas: space, organization, and signage. The store looked as though it should be twice its size, judging by the mountains of items piled on the shelves, hovering over me. I was like any person in a new environment. I tried to get my bearings and learn the system, but there didn't appear to be any system or organization. Signage for traffic-flow purposes was nonexistent. Where one aisle would have a small sign that named a few items in that particular row, the next aisle was signless. However, there was no lack of signage for advertisements. It was as if the workers at the store were demanded to hang, tape or fasten every single advertisement they were given from each company or product they sold. Cluttered down every aisle were multiple signs for Kelloggs, Gatorade, Crest, Campbells, Keebler, etc.

    I, of course, was in a general hurry and had only a few items to grab, but the sensory overload was dragging me into slow-down mode. My head swiveling, I took baby steps in search of direction. I looked at my short list and tried to chart a course. Just as I was getting started, an elderly woman with seemingly no awareness for others in the world around her cut right in front of me with her cart, nearly running over my toes. It was as if she was in a trance, and didn't even see me. I chuckled to myself and then noticed that I was easily half the age of most of the other customers.

    I trail-blazed ahead. I eventually secured my few items in an amazingly inefficient twenty-five minutes and began to make my way to one of only two checkout lines that appeared to be open. As I began to step to my spot in line, I again experienced the familiar gust of wind as an older woman with a shopping cart swooshed by. It was the same oblivious woman as before and she still didn't acknowledge her blatant cutoff as she moved in front of me in line. And that wasn't all: She had a shopping cart loaded with items and the elderly person behind the register began moving through them in super-slow motion.

Staring at the time ticking away and the measly four items in my hands, I began to get frustrated. I was fixated on this woman in front of me. Her clueless nature baffled me, and I deplored her unmistakably grouchy vibes with every movement she made. Time ticked and my frustration grew.

Just at the height of my frustration and with my eyes searching for even the smallest opening in the other checkout line, a woman with a passing cart stopped and called out to the grouchy woman.

"How's Kenny?" the passerby questioned.

"Not good," mumbled the grouch. "The cancer is going downhill, and I'm late getting to the hospital."

My brain stopped and my heart staggered. I had been so focused on my agenda and the obstacles slowing down my pursuits that I was the one who was in a trance. Why was I letting myself get so frustrated with this scene? Why was I reluctant to give the woman the benefit of the doubt? Was I in more of a hurry than she was? No. Did I have anything on my plate as heavy as hers? No. My perspective was altered in an instant and my frustrations melted away. I walked to my car ashamed of how I had allowed a simple shopping trip to frustrate me. It was a great reminder of all those others in the world who are in a much bigger hurry than I.

We never know what baggage those traveling beside us are carrying. We never know what is going on beneath the surface of the person sitting across from us at the conference table. I strive every day now to assume the best, even when people act the worst. I strive to believe in people even when I'm challenged by them. I strive to continually check the level of "hurries" in my life and keep them in perspective. And because of all that, when the ding goes off on the airplane, I choose to be still and let those in a true hurry go before me. Join me.

Questions For Your Journey . . .

Being Still at the 'Ding' in Your Organization

Finding time for stillness is essential to everyday life. If the ding of your alarm clock propels you into a sprint to check your e-mail, make your first phone call, book your next appointment, get your kids frantically off to school, or just enter into the same mundane morning routine as yesterday, consider beginning your day with just fifteen minutes of silence. A few moments of **conscious stillness** *in the midst of a world of stimulation allows us to bring our full selves to the events of our day. Beginning a day with deep breaths, thoughts of gratitude, prayer, or just quiet moments will bring perspective. When we are hurried, jumping from task to task, only looking to the next thing on our to-do list, the excellence and authenticity of our work suffers. We fly right past people and situations that are in need of greater attention. If you find yourself racing throughout your day, make a conscious effort to slow down and get out of the business of just doing and into the business of being excellent.*

- What areas of my life are speeding too fast?
- What type of leader do I aspire to be?
- Could a change of pace bring excellence to my work?
- In what way(s) can I be still at the ding in life today?

You Are Now Free to Move about the Cabin
Practice Stillness in This Moment

Notes

Step Back from the Baggage Claim

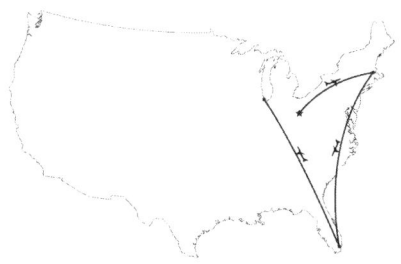

"People will forget what you said, people will forget what you did, but people will never forget how you made them feel."
- Maya Angelou

Seat 16 F: *Ministry of Availability*

FORTY-FIVE MINUTES OF SLEEP on a dirty baggage-claim-area floor and two hours on a fifteen-inch-wide pew in an empty airport chapel is not the quality of sleep most doctors recommend. Sleep was quite elusive throughout this adventure, so it left plenty of time to roam the corridors, people watch, and become very familiar with the airport's facilities.

Roughly thirty hours into my 160-hour, cross-country airplane tour, I decided it was time to take a short break from jotting down observations and pounding away on my computer. Ending the evening with a beer might help me get off to a better Night Two. Plus, with about six dollars left of my twenty-dollar daily allotment of spending money, I felt things were falling into place.

I sidled up to the bar at the Samuel Adams restaurant in the Terminal C ticketing area of Boston's Logan International Airport. A Boston Celtics game was on TV, so I enjoyed the opportunity to relax, take in some hoops, and make small talk with the bartender. Minutes after I took my seat at the bar, a tall, mustached man in his late-forties took the seat next to me.

"They servin' f#*%ing drinks at dis bar?" he questioned me.

"Yeah, that's the guy you want," I playfully gestured to the bartender.

"Hey, barkeep," he yelled down to the gray-haired man at the other end of the bar. "You servin' any f#*%ing drinks here tonight?" This guy was off to a great start.

"Yeah . . . I serve 'em from time to time," the bartender played along.

"Well, then how about a f#*%ing vodka and cranberry?" he barked out.

"Them Patriots are pretty f#*%ing good, aren't they?" he turned to me and asked. I was already getting used to his style of male communication. "Who you like this weekend?" he continued before I could answer his first question.

His name was Jack. Over the course of the next hour, he and I were bantering buddies. In between comments about the Celtics game and predictions for the weekend's football playoffs, I learned a couple of things about him. He was born and raised on an apple farm in New Hampshire. Growing up, farming was all he knew. They didn't have a lot of money, but his family worked hard and lived off the farm. He now lives in Florida, and works as a maintenance man for a very wealthy condo community.

"It's a great f#*%ing gig," he said. "I told my wife we'd be outta our freakin' minds to give this job up. I rake some of the f#*%ing yards every once in awhile, maybe clean some shutters, and they give me a f#*%ing huge Christmas bonus. It's perfect."

Jack had a lot of energy and, even though he was a bit brash, he was very playful and likable. I think he liked me, too. He wanted to know about my wife and kids, and the sincerity with which he simply said "that's great," when I told him how lucky I was, spoke more than those two words.

"You know, my father just had a f#*%ing stroke," he abruptly threw on the table. "That's why I'm here . . . I'm going to see my dad."

Silence. In a matter of seconds, the entire nature of our encounter changed. Jack went on to tell me the history of his father's health, the fact that his dad told him he didn't have to come visit, and how his family was responding. He talked, and I listened. Halfway through talking about his family, he called the bartender over and ordered two more drinks; one was for me. He continued for maybe thirty minutes until he looked at his watch and realized he needed to go.

"Jason, best of luck to you and tell those kids of yours I said 'hey'," he said in his playful way.

"Jack, I hope everything goes well with your dad," I said as we rose from our stools and shook hands. "It was nice meeting you."

As Jack walked out of the bar, I couldn't help but replay the last hour in my head. I don't think Jack came into that bar expecting to talk about his family's situation. For some reason, though, he needed to share it. I thought back to my reaction and wondered whether I should have offered him some wonderful Dr. Phil-type advice or attempted some sage wisdom regarding the challenges of life. The more I pondered the more I realized words were not what Jack was looking for or needing. He needed a body, a presence, someone who was just available to listen. I don't think he knew it or would articulate it that way—but for some reason, it was time for him to blurt it out. It was time to share his feelings with someone. I just happened to be that someone.

Step Back from the Baggage Claim

That night and into the next morning in the Boston airport I still thought about Jack and our encounter. The drool on my forearm and the glare from the fluorescent lights woke me. I lifted my head from the table in the food court of Terminal C and the clock on the wall read 3:23 a.m. My sight was blurry with exhaustion due to unconventional short stints of sleeping in so many awkward places. I scanned the empty concourse and Jack was still on my mind. I thought about the opportunities we all have to extend compassion to the people we randomly bump into in our lives. Family and friends are supposed to care, but a stranger—that's different. Somehow Jack knew I cared. Somehow Jack sensed I was available.

I made my rounds through the airport again that morning. I watched the chaotic scene at the baggage claim (it never gets old); I watched the security lines; I watched the airport workers; I listened to conversations. All the while, I took notes and kept thinking. I often found myself watching a specific person or group and wondered where they were headed. I tried to figure it out based on their baggage or clothing or hints in their conversations; so many interesting lives going in so many different directions.

That same morning I spotted a Latin American group of about fifteen people huddled together and sobbing. They were standing right at the start of the security line and the entire group was not just crying—they were sobbing. The beginning of the security line was so close to where one of the outside doors led to the streetside curb that it was a tight space for so many people to gather. People were trying to enter the security line, others were just entering or leaving the airport and, in the meantime, this poor family was trying to say their painful goodbyes. There were adults, teenage kids, and elementary age kids in the group—all crying. I was sucked into the intensity of their huddle. I tried to imagine who they were saying goodbye to and what their tragic situation was. Did someone pass away? Was someone in the military and heading overseas? With the depth of passion they were all sharing, I figured it had to be tragic.

As the group split in two, and half of them entered the security line, I watched them continue to sob uncontrollably. I knew I had to step outside of my comfort zone on this one. The easier thing would have been to walk away, but in the spirit of this adventure, I sucked up my uneasiness and approached the remainder of the group.

"Excuse me," I started. "I know it is none of my business and you certainly do not need to share anything with me if you do not want to, but I am curious to know who you were saying goodbye to."

"My sister's family," the mother replied in between sniffles. "They are from Australia and we won't see them for at least another three years."

"They were just visiting?" I asked.

"Yes, they were here for Christmas, but now are headed back home. Three years at least," she mumbled through her tears. "We won't see them for three years."

"I'm sorry to hear that," I said as we looked each other in the eyes one last time, wished each other well, and then continued in our different directions.

I'm not a crier, but as I walked away, tears welled in my eyes. The depth of this family's love caused me to imagine not seeing my brother's or sister's family for three years. I imagined our kids growing up apart, the minimal role we would play in each other's lives, the significant life moments we would miss, and the small amount of time we would have to share. I was struck by the complex logistics and distances that keep so many loved ones apart.

I sat on the plastic bench to the side of the security line and watched as person after person came in and out of the automated sliding doors leading to the street. So many people made their way through that doorway that it was almost a joke that a door actually existed there. The automated door would be only half-closed before it would whisk back open for a new traveler. I was reminded of how every single person flowing in and out of those doors also has a similarly intense set of emotions for people in their lives. They all have loved ones that are on their minds and in their hearts right now. It's not as though we are ticking time bombs of emotions walking around, but we are human beings with deeply embedded connections and love. What an absolute gift it is when we are able to be present physically and emotionally with those we love. How lucky we are to be available to care.

About two years ago I was led to the book *Improv Wisdom* by Patricia Ryan Madson. In the book, Madson discusses the art of improvisational comedy and the necessary skills that we all can use to live our lives with improvisation. She uses the following story to illustrate the skills an improviser uses to help someone who is struggling on stage.

> There's a Zen koan [teaching riddle] about two monks walking along an embankment in the dead of winter. A blizzard rages, and the snow is deep. The elder monk slips off the narrow path and falls ten feet into a snowy crevasse. The younger monk assesses the circumstance and sees that there is no way to pull his friend to safety. The koan asks what the young monk should do. The answer to this puzzle is that the young monk should jump into the abyss with his fellow monk. Sometimes the only thing we can do is to join the suffering of others—to be there alongside them. There is no fix, no remedy. But we dare not leave our comrade in distress.

I'll never forget walking into my home during my freshmen year in high school. My mom came into my room just as I was throwing my backpack on my bed. I'll never forget her puffy eyes as she asked me to sit on the bed. I'll never forget her holding my hand and carefully explaining to me that my grandfather had just committed suicide. I'll never forget the flood of confusion, sadness, frustration, and questions that ensued.

Not long after his death, I went to some kind of gathering for high school students. I can't tell you anything about the program that night. The only thing I can remember is that I stood outside of the gathering space with one of the volunteer adult leaders, the legendarily quirky, Mark Buchsieb. Mark was a slender man in his forties at the time, who routinely wore a "No Whining" T-shirt, and would fake falls in public just to get a rise out of people. This night the two of us just stood there together. I can't tell you anything he said specifically about my grandfather (although I know he did). I can't tell you anything that I shared about my grandfather or how I was feeling (although I know I did). What I can remember is him standing with me, being fully present with me. He was practicing what he referred to as our "ministry of availability" to those around us. The opportunity to just care for people; not doctrine or words—care. He understood that I didn't need words that night or someone to try to fix my feelings. He understood that all he needed to do was jump down into that abyss and just be with me. And so he did.

Mama Carmen and Papa Jorge

When my cell phone rang in the fall of 2003 and Jorge Gonzalez from Tijuana, Mexico, was on the line, I couldn't have predicted how much that call was going to affect my life. During our Mexico mission trip the previous March, our group of nearly 200 high school students, college students, and adults built twelve houses for families who had been living in shacks. By chance, one of our work teams met Jorge. He walked a small group up to see the orphanage and handed the adult leaders of that group his business card, which they passed on to me back at our campsite. The next January, my wife and I were on a plane to see the orphanage. It was a remarkable turn of events, which caused our lives to merge.

Over ten years ago, Carmen Gonzalez felt God was calling her to a higher purpose. One morning she said to her husband Jorge, pastor of their local church, "God is telling me to take kids off of the streets. He wants me to start an orphanage."

"You'd better pray a bit more on that one," Jorge replied with big eyes and his usual sense of humor.

Sure enough, Carmen felt a deep calling to open an orphanage and care for the kids of Tijuana who were abandoned or afflicted with traumatic childhoods. Her goal the first year was to house eight boys and eight girls in the "orphanage"—a fancy term for their house. The great need as well as her generous loving spirit caused the project to snowball. Now, years later, in a completely different (and, again, maxed-out) space, Carmen and Jorge Gonzalez and their family are the parents for over 110 orphans at the Casa Hogar Sion Orphanage. The six two-story stucco buildings leave only a little room for narrow cement paths leading to each building. They have expanded so much on the land they have that only a small common area exists for playground and parking purposes. In the evening the dark backdrop of the mountain range contrasts with the lights of Tijuana and San Diego, providing a unique backdrop for this magical place.

From the first moment I stepped foot on their property, it was apparent that this ministry of availability was built on the firm foundation of God's love for all people. Their compassion for the kids was striking, their humility endearing, and their deflection of any credit or praise was uncommonly genuine. "This is God's orphanage," Carmen insists, "We don't own it."

Our friendship has grown over the past seven years, and I've done every thing I could to visit them at least two, three, sometimes even four times a year. Carmen's words, spoken on one of our early trips to the orphanage with high school students, still echo in my heart.

"We had three new babies just come to the orphanage," she began as our group of sixteen students gathered in a tight circle around her.

> The first baby: The mother had the baby in the hospital, then put her clothes on, and snuck out of the hospital. The second baby: The mother had the baby in the hospital, put her clothes back on, walked out the front door, set the baby on the ground, and disappeared into the streets. The third baby: The mother had the baby in the hospital, put her clothes back on, walked out the front door, placed the baby in the dumpster, and walked away.

A heavy weight of sadness, anger, and confusion lingered amidst the silence of the group. Teary eyes and tighter grips pulled the group closer together. The aching silence continued. Just when our grief for those babies was about to reach its full depth, a different image emerged. Over Carmen's shoulder we could see kids dashing to the makeshift playground and hear echoes of laughing play. All of a sudden, it was abundantly clear. Thank God there are people who are willing to go into the dumpsters of this world. Thank God for a loving and compassionate spirit that reaches the unimaginable depths of humanity. Thank

God for those whose ministry of availability has nothing to do with their words and everything to do with their presence. Thank God those babies found their way to this place. I'm sure some of those 110 orphans can recall some of the loving words Mama Carmen and Papa Jorge spoke to them during the horrific times in their abandoned lives. Even more significantly, I guarantee every single one of them knows exactly how they made them feel in those moments. They felt Carmen and Jorge's willingness to be there for them—their desire to jump down into that abyss with them has made all the difference in their lives.

    We have no idea what tugs at the hearts of the people we sit next to on the airplane, stand next to in the security lines, bump into in the food court, or box out at the baggage claim. We're clueless about the gifts, expertise, and talents of those individuals, just as we are clueless about what is challenging, haunting, or painful in those exact moments in their lives. We cannot possibly know or understand the unique challenges in the lives of strangers, but I do believe that awareness serves us. It serves the world to be aware that others may be hurting inside. It serves the world to see strangers with compassionate eyes. And, it serves the world that when someone is aching, whether we know them or not, we are available to just be there with them.

In our organizational lives, there are always opportunities to put this spirit into action. There are critical times to remind those we work with that their life as a human-being is more important than just the things they 'do' for us. As leaders, we have to remember the simple words from management gurus Ken Blanchard and Spencer Johnson in their national bestselling book *The One Minute Manager*, "People who feel good about themselves produce good results." Imagine what kind of organizations we can create when caring for people becomes our highest value. It doesn't matter whether you're a part of a Fortune 500 company or your own small business - when you cultivate authentic, caring relationships you'll produce good results.

Let's make a commitment to start this ministry of availability in the airports we visit and then let that generous, compassionate spirit spill over into the business meetings, grocery stores, coffee shops, gyms, schools, churches, offices, and streets in our lives. In the precious moments along our shared journey, a few moments of wordless compassion from a stranger can make all the difference in our world.

Questions For Your Journey . . .
Availability in Your Organization

How often do we dive into the minutiae of our everyday lives but know very little about the person in the cubicle next to us at work, the client on the other end of that email, our next door neighbors, the person sitting in the same pew at church, the parents at our child's little league game, or someone in our very own family? Every single person in this world operates at a higher level in all facets of their life when they feel valued, affirmed, celebrated, challenged, and cared for. It isn't realistic to believe that you will be best friends with everyone you come into contact with, but being available and learning about what is important to them makes a profound impact. The best teammates, leaders, and friends, and most successful people I have observed not only bring their expertise to the table, but connect, value, and are available to the people around them. Even when courageous conversations are called for with someone on your staff, commit to sitting in the same room and sharing dignity, respect, and compassion. The spirit that you carry every day to "how" and "why" you do your work does make a significant contribution to the culture you help create in your organization. Each action you put out into the world impacts the culture of the space around you.

*Today, don't just show up—**be available**. If someone is hurting, don't try to solve it, just jump down in the abyss and be with them. Take time to connect with the person who is on the other side of that conference table or planning session. Go out of your way to be an available presence for those on your team. We can't always chart the value of these efforts in regards to the bottom line, but trust your intuition that caring for people always adds value to the world. When you're available, who knows the significance you can bring to the person on the other end of that next phone call, email or conversation in the parking lot. And, in practicing your ministry of availability throughout your day, I guarantee you'll be better at the job you're being asked to do. The most important task you may accomplish today is allowing yourself to step away from your computer when a colleague in need shows up at your door.*

- Who in my organization needs my ministry of availability?
- When has someone jumped down into the abyss with me during a challenging time in my career?
- Has a stranger, client, or teammate ever surprised me with a small gesture of compassion?
- In what way(s) can I practice the ministry of availability today?

Ministry of Availability
Share Compassion with Those Along Your Journey

Notes

"**L**eadership Begins With Availability."

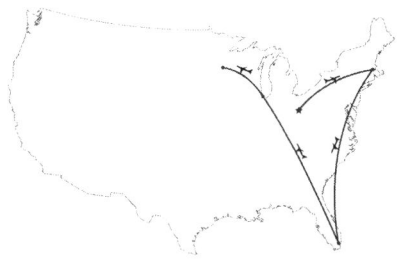

"We can throw stones, complain about them, stumble on them, climb over them, or build with them."
- William Arthur Ward

Choose Your Own Adventure

WHEN I WAS A KID, *Choose Your Own Adventure* books were extremely popular. They were innovative for kids. Imaginative, exciting, and participatory—everything a growing kid enjoys! Originally published from 1979 to 1998 by Bantam Books, they went on to become one of the most successful children's book series of all time.

They were written in second-person. For example, there might be a story about a cross-country bicycle race (work with me on this; I don't remember any of the exact plots of the books, but the concept is imaginative) when, all of a sudden, the reader would have a choice to make regarding which path the character would take. To choose the path to the left (a gravel road), turn to page 46. To choose the path to the right (a steep incline ahead), turn to page 61. Or, to choose the off-road dirt path (that appears to be a shortcut), turn to page 77. Each option provided only partial information on which to assess the situation.

For an imaginative child, the exercise was exhilarating. The reader had to make decisions for the adventure to continue. The amusing thing about the decision was, without fail, after reading only a few pages of your chosen path, you were peeking back to see how the other options would have played out. You just had to compare your choice with the other paths. Once you finished one path in its entirety, you felt compelled to go back and read how the other scenarios played out. Some paths that seemed exciting at first didn't end up being the wildest stories. Some paths that at first appeared to be the safe, boring routes, were in fact the ones that ended with a thrilling twist. And, like every good story, a surprise was always around the corner. Throughout the entire adventure, you were constantly comparing the different paths and the different outcomes with your choices.

As I stare at the jam-packed security lines at Miami International Airport, I can't help but compare life to one big *Choose Your Own Adventure* story. Just like someone coming to the abrupt end of one of those moving walkways where their body stumbles for a second in order to return to a slower pace, the bustling crowd approaches the security lines with a fury, but then jolts into a slower gear. Each individual weaves in and out of the rope lines until they reach the point in the security line where it breaks up into three, four, five, even up to eight different paths leading to the x-ray machines. You can see the agonizing look creep across some people's faces as they are forced to make a quick decision regarding their path; perhaps a flashback to their own *Choose Your Own Adventure* days.

The pressure's on, so they have to gather as much information as they quickly can. These are the moments that Malcolm Gladwell in his bestselling book *Blink* refers to as "thin slicing"—those instantaneous intuitions that our brains accomplish in the blink of an eye. We're surveying the number of people in each line, the pace of the TSA workers leading each path, searching for those passengers who will undoubtedly slow each line. All of these judgments are made in an instant, and we make our choice.

With a step into one of the lines, we peek back to some of the other pages just to see where we might have been if we had chosen a different path. We pick out someone in the other security line that we almost selected and use them as our measuring stick. With each twist of the line or new person going through the x-ray machine, our head bounces back and forth from line to line to see if we made the right choice. It's a constant comparison—the choice in our life playing out right in front of us.

When we reach the x-ray machine two or three persons ahead of our counterpart, we're ecstatic. Call it competition. Call it mental gambling. Or, call it obsession with making the so-called "right" choices in life and selecting the so-called "best" path. Either way, it seems to affect us. When our counterpart reaches his x-ray machine two or three people ahead of us because of the totally disorganized family who didn't bother to fold up their stroller until they reached the front of the line, we've lost the game. We sit and stew, annoyed that our line is taking so long. "I already would have been through the line by now if I had just chosen the other path!"

Comparisons are everywhere in our culture, and we're very good at them. We know everything there is to know about keeping up with the people next door. We know what the cool kids are wearing at school, what car the president of the company drives, who in our group of friends got married first, who makes the most money, whose family has the best vacation home, and how thin the hottest celebrity du jour is.

It isn't rocket science to point out how immersed we are in a culture of comparison. We look back on decisions we made earlier in life and evaluate how they impact us today. We focus intently on our next step or the series of choices needing to be made at this stage in life and wonder where they will take us. The fact is, we spend an awful lot of time thinking about how we landed where we are—and probably even more energy trying to predict what will come next. All the while, do we fully appreciate and enjoy the only unique moment we have, right now? Do we stand in the security line and figure out a way to enjoy the wait? Do we turn to the people on either side and take the opportunity to meet someone new? Do we reflect on how privileged we are to be able to travel to wherever we are heading no matter how enjoyable or painful our trip's purpose may be? Especially in today's world of high fuel prices and many flight delays or cancellations, a calming patience is needed for all the obstacles along our journey that are out of our control. In the thick of the delays of life, is it possible to pause and say thank you for the life we have right now?

Refrigerator Man

I remember the night I met "The Refrigerator Man" for the first time. We had recently begun what would soon become known as our weekly *Streets Mission Project*. Each Thursday night, high school students, dedicated adults, and college students would come together to package individual dinners and necessary supplies such as blankets, hats, and gloves to deliver to homeless people living on the streets of Columbus.

In the beginning, a group of five-to-twenty volunteers would deliver twenty meals to spots under bridges, in the woods, or by the railroad tracks downtown. From the program's beginning in the winter of 1999, the participation has grown. Up to sixty high school students may be involved, and the group now delivers about 120 meals weekly.

The mission remains simple:
- Feed the hungry; clothe the cold
- Share dignity and respect with all
- Love one another

It was a frigid Thursday night in the winter of 1999 when our small crew headed down to the streets again and, this time, met a new friend. We set out on our route to the various "camps" (that is how the homeless community refers to their homes). Because many of the camps were old rotted shanties in the woods, tents hidden among the trees, or other makeshift creations by the railroad tracks, we would drive as far as we could and then set out on foot. The typical scene would consist of a pile of dirty blankets, surrounded by a smattering of trash, tucked out of sight under a bridge or behind a building. More advanced camps had a small tent or lean-to constructed of wooden crates and rotted lumber hidden behind the trees, with the city skyline in the background. As we finished delivering a meal and visiting with some of our friends who happened to live in an abandoned RV trailer in the woods, they asked if we had met "The Refrigerator Man"? We were intrigued, and so they pointed us in the direction of this supposed character.

We trounced through the snow, weaving in and out of trees in a wooded area just south of downtown. It always amazed me how we could be just a couple blocks from the heart of downtown, yet hidden in a forest. After a couple of minutes, we came to what appeared to be an old refrigerator lying on its side in the snow in the middle of the woods. Our small group held back about twenty feet as I approached the box and yelled out, "Is anyone in there? We've got food." A moment later, a foot poked out of what was the freezer portion of the refrigerator, and I soon stood face-to-face with a man.

I introduced myself and he said, "My name is John, but everyone around here seems to call me 'Refrigerator Man.'" He was a short man, maybe five-feet-seven, with a mustache and glasses. We handed him a meal for which he was very grateful, and also made sure he was warm enough.

"This refrigerator is a gift," he began in an excited voice. "It keeps me warm and I'm so thankful I found it because if I hadn't, I'd be lying on the ground."

The high school students and adults standing behind me during this encounter fought back tears. We were in awe that someone was actually living like this in the dead of winter in Columbus, Ohio, and we were in even greater awe of his gratitude. He assured us he was okay and we promised him we'd see him next week.

We went on to know John, aka Refrigerator Man, for a few years after that night. He soon built his own little wooden shanty in the woods and we saw him each week. Counter to the many generalizations you hear about the homeless, each person I met on the streets was a completely different person with a unique story. Sure, sometimes there were common threads, but to claim to understand the complexity of homelessness and to tie it up in one general statement as some people do is extremely inaccurate, in my experience.

The Refrigerator Man was especially unique. Quite often I would end a Thursday night wondering why he was living in a box in the woods. He spent most days at the library reading anything he could get his hands on. He was resourceful, as many who live on the land are, but he didn't seem to have any vices. He welcomed three or four stray cats into his home and took great pride in providing for them. He liked to keep to himself, to do his own thing, and enjoyed where he was in life. One day he was gone and I never heard where he went.

I like to believe that, if nothing else, the friendship, respect, and care he received from our group over the years made it a little easier for him to make whatever next move he chose to make. I'll never forget his infectious gratitude that first night we met. He never spoke or lamented about the right or wrong turns he took in the past or worried over his next plan of attack. He did not complain about his spot in life or focus on what he did not have. He was grateful for what he did have, fully embraced where he was in the "security line," and chose to be grateful along the way. I think about his spirit often.

A few years ago, I was sitting out in front of Mama Carmen and Papa Jorge's house in Tijuana. Some of my favorite moments while visiting include sitting outside with a cup of coffee early in the morning. Typical in Tijuana, the small crowded property lots are lined with chain-link fence to protect the small area they have to claim. The early morning scene often includes many disheveled stray dogs roaming the trash-filled dirt streets, yapping back and forth at each other. This may not seem like a relaxing environment but, to me, coupled with the mountains in the background, is a beautiful departure from my norm.

This particular morning it was raining. In many parts of Mexico this presents unique challenges due to dirt streets that quickly become mud pits. Vehicles fight to make even slight progress and, therefore, plans for the day are abandoned. I sat with my cup of coffee, the rest of our group snuggled away upstairs on the floor in their sleeping bags, the sound of rain sprinkling the roof top, and watched a young family walking slowly through the mud. The young mother and father were attempting to navigate their double-stroller through the sloppy mud. Two children (ages about one and three), sat quietly in the stroller as they were jostled back and forth from their father sliding them through the mud. The third child (about four years of age) was holding the mother's left hand, and the mother carried a small bag of groceries in her right hand. It was obvious they had just been down the street to the local mercado to get some needed supplies in anticipation of their rained-in day.

    The kids laughed at one another and the parents giggled back and forth as they approached their house. They unlocked their chain-link fence and made their way into their small two-room home. As I watched this scene, I wondered what the day ahead of them entailed. The father probably worked at one of the local manufacturing plants for less than fifteen dollars a day. I imagined that not being able to get to his job was not a good thing. I wondered what missing out on that day's pay would mean to a family that was already scraping by with so little. Still, the look on their faces and way they responded to each other didn't suggest frustration or complaint. They appeared to be taking the path they were given for this day gracefully and heading inside to enjoy the time as a family.

I must admit, as they disappeared into their house, I was strangely envious. I was imagining what it would take back home to keep a parent from going to work (and ours would probably still be paid)! What would our attitude be in the midst of that deviation from our daily routine? Would we give ourselves the freedom to gracefully accept the altered path and make the most of it no matter what the changed circumstances meant? Would we see the changed circumstances as an opportunity to do something unique with our loved ones or would we complain about our bad luck and fill our time with unnecessary tasks? How would we deal with the obstacles along our path? After the initial feeling of envy for this family, I realized we all have the choice to welcome whatever today brings. We all have the opportunity to enter into what David L. Goetz in his book *Death By Suburb* refers to as a final soul practice: "To fall in love with a day." No matter what obstacles appear in the security lines of our life, we all have the ability to fall in love right where we find ourselves.

As I watch each person select their line in Miami's version of the "security line adventure," I can't help but wonder how we could learn to enjoy our wait. As each person's eyes incessantly gravitate toward their watch to check the time, rush to consume the last bit of water or coffee before they reach the checkpoint, or stare obsessively at the fast moving line they should have chosen, are they ever truly present in that moment? I wonder if the person behind them is an expert in some subject and they are missing out on this one-chance meeting opportunity. Perhaps the person ahead of them has a story that will make life today feel totally unique. Is there a way to be fully present, even in the waiting moments of life?

If you haven't seen the 1997 film *Life Is Beautiful* and dare to deal with the range of emotions this story releases, go rent it today. This tragic love story, cleverly written with comedic zest, is about Guido, Jewish–Italian father (played by Roberto Benigni, who also co-wrote and directed the film) and his five-year-old son who are deported to a concentration camp during WWII. The movie does not diminish the horror of the concentration camps, but it does deal with them in a poetic way.

Without giving away specifics (again, you really should watch the film!), Guido convinces his young son that the concentration camp is actually an elaborate role-playing game in which the "prisoners" are competing for points in the hope of winning a real battle tank. It sounds too unbelievable, but the way the story unfolds is remarkable. The metaphor reminds us of the great capacity we all have to love those around us and the beauty that can radiate from our lives even in the most tragic and restricted situations. If you have seen it, you know the true beauty of this story shines because of the way life is embraced and celebrated even in the midst of some of the darkest circumstances. It makes you wish you could bring one-tenth of the positive spirit and faith witnessed in the movie to life in the trivial experiences that challenge us daily.

When reminded of those horrific stories in the history of mankind or the everyday faces of people who are struggling with traumatic realities, our place in the security line suddenly doesn't seem that significant. Those images provide us perspective on our own lives and allow us to feel better about where we are. So what if we are two spots further back in the line than we thought we would be? So what if there is another delay? So what if life doesn't seem to be playing out exactly the way we had hoped? After all, with the big picture of our lives in mind, we're still okay, right?

Everyone right now is experiencing the security line wait in some form in their lives away from the airport. The security line you are waiting in right now in your life may include the promotion at work you are hoping for, the impending sale of your house, your upcoming wedding, your stressful divorce, the terminal illness of a loved one, the wait following a college application, the hopeful outcome of a complicated pregnancy, a retirement that is just around the corner, the job offer you hope to receive, or just the delayed flight you are experiencing right now in the airport. How we handle the wait at the security line in the airport does spill over into the other lines in our lives. This doesn't mean we don't ever experience frustration, sadness or disappointment due to an obstacle along our path, but rather, we learn to rely on our gratitude within to handle those instances. Learning to gracefully handle the delays in our traveling journeys prepares us to be able to adapt to the inevitable change that all experience in life. Thankfully, folks in our past, or those walking beside us today have shown us that we can not just handle the trials in life, but thrive!

Cast Down Your Bucket Where You Are!

Booker T. Washington described himself as a "representative of the Negro Race" when he delivered his 1895 Cotton States Exposition address chronicled in Chapter 14 of his book *Up From Slavery*. Washington was born into slavery, freed at the age of nine, and went on to become educated, an author and leader within the African American community and our country. As he stood to deliver his Exposition address, he admitted that "uppermost in my mind was the desire to say something that would cement the friendship of the races and bring about hearty cooperation between them." One of his illustrations from that address sends a message to all of us about moving forward to change the world.

Step Back from the Baggage Claim

A ship lost at sea for many days suddenly sighted a friendly vessel. From the mast of the unfortunate vessel was seen a signal, 'Water, water; we die of thirst!' The answer from the friendly vessel at once came back, 'Cast down your bucket where you are.' A second time the signal, 'Water, water; send us water!' ran up from the distressed vessel, and was answered, 'Cast down your bucket where you are.' And a third and a fourth signal for water were answered, 'Cast down your bucket where you are.' The captain of the distressed vessel, at last heeding the injunction, cast down his bucket, and it came up full of fresh, sparkling water from the mouth of the Amazon River. To those of my race who depend on bettering their condition in a foreign land or who underestimate the importance of cultivating friendly relations with the Southern white man, who is their next- door neighbour, I would say: 'Cast down your bucket where you are.' Cast it down in making friends in every manly way of the people of all races by whom we are surrounded.

His message was loud and clear to all. If you want to see change in your life, the only thing you can do is cast your bucket down where you are. The only way to perpetuate progress was to throw all of your efforts and energy into working hard, living, educating, and stepping closer to one another right where you are. There wasn't going to be a "silver bullet" solution that would erase all in our history that led us to this point. In a world of racial inequities, change had to start with each individual in the communities and cities they inhabited. They couldn't wait for their circumstances to change around them; it was their time to live with great joy and passion where they were.

To this day, even with as much progress as many have made, each of us still has a daily choice about how we can cast down our bucket and live fully where we are. There is still progress to be made. Hearing those words today encourages each of us (no matter what race or background) to live to our full potential right where we are. There still is no "flip of the switch" answer to our challenges nor perfect place to which we can escape. The surest way to change the world we are experiencing right now is to "cast down our bucket where we are."

When I was in second grade, my family lived in Cairo, Egypt. My father is an international businessman and, at that time, was engaged in a number of projects in the Middle East. Rather than being away from us for long stretches of time, my parents jumped at the opportunity for our family to live overseas that school year. The daily routine, sights, sounds, and smells in a foreign land were quite different from suburban Columbus, Ohio. The intense, wonderful experiences of that year are more deeply embedded in me than I know.

For the last few months of our stay in Egypt, we lived in a tall apartment complex. From the inside window of our living room, you could look down the fifteen-foot-diameter air shaft that ran through the inside of the building. I remember standing at the windowsill one day and staring down into the hollow chasm. I could see, at the very bottom of the shaft, a few sheets hung up like tarps. As I looked more closely, I noticed there were people down there. When I asked my mom what those people were doing down there, the answer was one that I still am trying to wrap my brain around:

"That is the apartment manager's family, Jason," my mom explained gently. "The man who takes care of this building. That is where he and his family live."

For months we had been running around in the dirt streets outside the building playing soccer with his young boys. They were always so happy and fun playmates. I couldn't understand how we got to live in such a nice place and their family lived down there. After all, we were just visiting and this would always be their home. Nearly thirty years later, I still think about how inequitable the world is. Why was I so lucky to be born into my family? How come our lives would be so drastically different based on the geography of our births? I didn't do anything to deserve the nice apartment, and that Egyptian family didn't do anything to deserve living in the air shaft. I've realized over the years that it doesn't accomplish anything for either of us to feel guilty or bitter about the hand we were dealt. The only way to fully appreciate the lives we have is to live with joy and gratitude where we are. I see the smiles and happiness on the faces of those boys as we played soccer in the dirt, and I'm inspired and reminded: The very best of life arrives when we decide to cast down our bucket where we are.

I spent the night roaming throughout the Miami airport. My 90 minutes of sleep came while I was curled up on the shiny airport floor as dozens of professional cleaners drove floor-waxing machines that looked like bumper cars. It looked like a fun way to enjoy the night shift at the airport. As the 5 a.m. security lines in Miami began to transform into a sea of people, early-morning moods were apparent on the faces of the anxious travelers. The rising steam from hundreds of passing coffee cups signaled the official start to a new day and the next opportunity to gracefully handle whatever comes their way. Stranger after stranger hustled into the security maze searching for the best path to guide them out the other end as quickly as possible. There is no perfect path, but always the opportunity to enjoy the journey.

Booker T. Washington's words still ring true today. The inequities and imperfections we experience in our own lives today are not going to be solved by comparing ourselves to those on either side of us or complaining about what led us to this particular spot in life. True progress and happiness in our lives is going to come from a commitment to make the most of the present moment. In our careers, it is so easy to become obsessed with looking for the next opportunity or worrying about how the future is going to play out that we miss the opportunity we have right now. We can easily get caught up in large staff structures and throw our hands in the air and say "things will never change". But, true leadership begins right where we are - choosing to impact the culture of the part of the organization that we're a part of. We may not be able to change the whole system, but we can impact the 'lines' we stand in.

We all have the opportunity, no matter where we stand in the lines of our lives, to make the most of where we are. Making the most of where we are may not translate into pure bliss, but it does adjust our lens slightly so that our angle of vision becomes focused on gratitude. Perhaps we can move beyond the comparisons and complaints of the security line and live fully within our path. In Ralph Waldo Emerson's words, "What lies behind us and what lies before us are tiny matters compared to what lies within us."

Today is just another "opportunity in line" for us to "cast down our bucket where we are." Today, cast down your bucket by doing something thoughtful for a neighbor you don't know very well, by expressing your gratitude to your staff, by spending a few intentional moments with a client, or by choosing to laugh during the five-o'clock traffic. Cast down your bucket by breathing deeply, enjoying where you are in line, and saying thank you for today.

Questions For Your Journey . . .
Choosing Now in Your Organization

*Ingrained deep within our culture is the idea that "the grass is always greener somewhere else." When we allow that mantra to continuously ring in the background of our lives we can become overly strategic in the plotting of our lives. Our eyes are focused directly on comparing ourselves to others. Our focus may become too concentrated on the future or the past and, in that process, our present lives suffer. If we can harness all of the energy that we spend making comparisons or futuristic thinking and focus on this present moment, we have a much better chance of thriving. When we thrive, opportunities arise. The only way to know whether there is a better road to travel is to first fully explore and live the path that we are on. Whatever "security line wait" you are experiencing right now in life, cast down your bucket where you are. Make the most of each moment and try your best to enjoy, appreciate, celebrate, and grow—**now**. Thrive by bringing a grateful and joyful spirit to life today.*

- To whom do I compare myself in life and business?
- What do I have to be grateful for?
- How can I celebrate today?
- How will I "cast down my bucket where I am"?

Choose Your Own Adventure
Quit the Comparison Game and Thrive Where You Are

Notes

Step Back from the Baggage Claim

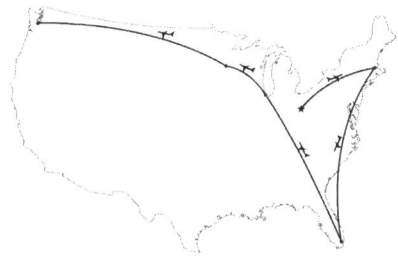

"Sometimes you gotta create what you want to be a part of."
- Geri Weitzman

Embrace *SkyMall*

WHO DOESN'T WANT A DOUGH-NU-MATIC appliance that spits out a dozen hot doughnuts in six minutes? How about an $899.95 portable, inflatable, whirlpool spa for those moments you could go for a hot soak? Or, better yet, don't you need a can of "Poop-Freeze," which sprays a liquefied gas that super-chills and hardens your dog's excrement in your yard to -62 degrees for easier pickup? Thank you, *SkyMall!*

SkyMall magazine, the airlines' gateway to shopping land, is one of the highlights of my airplane experience. On my flights from Miami to Chicago, and then Chicago to Minneapolis, nearly every person in my row spent at least fifteen minutes combing *SkyMall*. Like a rite of passage into every new flight, each traveler seemed almost to be beckoned by *SkyMall*. There appeared to be two standard modes of viewing: slowly browsing the catalog page-by-page and then hanging it up for the flight or revisiting it a couple of times during the flight for quick hunting. No matter how many times I look through that collection of neat, strange, wonderful, horrible, ridiculous items, I am fulfilled. On every flight I take, I leave at least a few minutes to leaf through *SkyMall* and enter their weird-o-world of creativity. Two of my all-time favorites (but seem to be getting phased out for some unknown reason) are the Hotdog Grill and Bun Warmer and that infamous airplane magazine advertisement for . . . the ROM!

The Hotdog Grill and Bun Warmer is pure genius. I'm not sure who out there is eating so many hotdogs that it necessitates having their very own appliance, but still, somebody saw an opening in the marketplace and filled it. The hotdog grill looks like a toaster, but instead of having the rectangular slits for bread, it has two holes for the hotdogs and two holes for the buns. For those households that are scarfing down hotdogs frequently, all they have to do is pull out the trusty hotdog grill, throw two in, wait a few minutes until they pop up, throw two more in, and repeat until all are fed. It is as easy as that and it even gives you one more appliance to take up space in the kitchen. All of that for the low price of $49.95.

A good friend of mine introduced me to the immaculate world of the ROM. The ROM requires its own full-page advertisement. The headline reads: "Exercise in exactly 4 minutes per day." Yes, only four minutes! And the ROM, which looks like some medieval torture device / stationary bicycle / jungle gym, can be yours for only $14,615. Yes, $14,615! The advertisement says 97 percent of the people who rent the ROM for a thirty-day trial decide to purchase it. At that price, I hope the 97 percent is somehow made up of just one person.

Believe it or not, I'm not making fun of these products, their creators or *SkyMall*. In fact, I hope you'll see I'm celebrating these products (for all I know, they are great products), these creators and, indeed, *SkyMall*. I love *SkyMall* and everything in it because to me it represents a world of whacked out creations, none of which are perfect. I love ideas. I've always joked with some of my friends that one of my goals in life is to be a part of a "think tank." I don't care what we're "think-tanking" about; I just love the idea of a space to let every idea fly. That is what I think *SkyMall* represents. It invites us to let our minds jump to even the strangest ideas, a time to wander creatively. I know I need that. Our world needs that.

As I've stated, my mind seems to be on overdrive when I'm on an airplane. *SkyMall* jump starts it, and my mind treasures the different pace I experience while on the flight. It is designated time when I have nowhere I possibly can go. I'm in my airline seat for as long as the flight takes. At this stage in technology, I can't easily make phone calls, I can't answer text messages, surf the Internet, exercise or run errands. I can, however, sit and let the ideas roll. Once I get past the feeling of being restricted and not having all of those items I just named, I actually enjoy it. I take the time to read something I've had on my list for awhile, I rest, or I just sit and think. I always have a pen with me and I always have a legal pad.

Like *SkyMall,* my legal pad of thoughts is open to any crazy idea, and by the end of my own creativity sessions, not all the ideas are worth following. In fact, some are horrible. But, the time and space to create is invaluable, and no matter whether the ideas are good or bad, they always lead to something (one idea was this book . . . I'll let you decide whether it was a good idea). I watch the pace that we all seem to be running in our lives and I know the first thing to be cut is creative time to explore. The time to create gets squelched by the demand to just get things done. If we are able to step back in our lives and gain perspective, slow down at the ding, and get away from the comparison game at the security lines, we open ourselves up to let our most creative work come out.

I wonder what it would mean for our own lives and for the world if we all embraced the *SkyMall* time of creativity on our flights and then let it spill over into our everyday lives. What would it mean for our lives if we were dedicated to setting aside time to just be, think, and create? I know so many people who complain about the routines of their lives and the culture at their workplaces that are stuck at the status quo—individuals, relationships, or organizations resorting daily to just doing things the way they did things yesterday. What would a new *SkyMall* mentality mean for our projects at work, our friendships and marriages, the teams we play on, the artistic hobbies we yearn for, or even our health? I wonder what could be created in a world where we celebrated and encouraged continuous ideas, even the bad ones. I wonder how a *SkyMall* culture of creativity in our individual lives could eventually spill over into solutions to the world's big issues such as terrorism, climate change, immigration, healthcare, poverty, or racism. I wonder.

Create On Demand

One of my practices of taking the *SkyMall* experience into my life has been listening to a podcast while I exercise. Giving my mind the space and freedom to run creatively while working out has made both more enjoyable. In the past, a podcast of choice for me has been "The Accidental Creative."

Todd Henry, the founder of "The Accidental Creative," refers to today's culture as "create on demand." The mission of the accidental creative is to encourage individuals to find their unique voices because "'cover bands' (bands that just play other people's music) do not change the world." Each podcast presents not only Henry's thoughts and experiences along his personal creative journey, but also interviews with other creatives in the world who are trying to produce vibrant work in a create-on-demand culture.

In podcast #90, Henry explains the process of creativity as he sees it:

> All creativity is ultimately accidental. It's not that we are not doing a lot of prep work to get to those breakthrough moments. It's that we can't really control what the smashing together of separate pieces of stimulus will produce. We can only (1) prepare ourselves by practicing some creative disciplines and (2) be prepared to recognize the emerging patterns as our work is developing. We need to be able to spot those creative accidents when they happen . . . What we need to learn to do is live with a creative ethic. To approach our lives in such a way that we're always open, we're always paying attention to stimulus, we're always smashing

things together so that creativity, whether necessary or not, is simply our way of living in this world.

The discipline that allows us the freedom and space to create puts us into a realm where ideas can begin, develop, grow, die if they need to, and spiral into whatever they may become. Without that space in our lives, we end up just going through the motions, zoning out, flipping on autopilot, following the status quo.

This is the point in this book where you become very interested in bamboo. (How's that for creativity?) Bamboo follows a growth structure that is quite different from other plants. The bamboo "canes," referred to as culms, grow from a branching underground root structure known as a rhizome (much like grass). The branching underground root structure grows only a short distance before another culm shoots off from it and continues the growth. Simply put, bamboo doesn't just grow individual canes straight into the air one at a time. The roots branch out sideways, each culm growing a short distance until it shoots off in another direction.

I believe our creative lives follow a pattern similar to that of bamboo. It is highly unlikely that one day we just decide we are going to be creative so we flip the switch and turn on our good ideas. We don't just start thinking about one idea and have our train of thought follow in one linear direction. Rather, we put ourselves into the frame of mind to practice some creative disciplines where thoughts can branch out, and then look to recognize when an offshoot of an original idea moves us in a better direction. In this discipline of continual creation, each idea (good or bad) serves a purpose and leads to the offshoot of something else. No idea stands purely on its own. Each creative burst perpetuates further growth. This point is important for me to remember because I often want to actualize every idea—yet that is impossible. Eventually through the branching of creative thought, one of the bamboo shoots is worth chasing. Maybe it looks like a hot dog warmer or maybe it looks entirely different!

So there I sat at the window seat of yet another airplane with *SkyMall* in hand. Flying west from Minneapolis into Seattle on a sunny day in January is breathtaking. It felt almost rude to not wake the sleeping passengers scattered throughout the plane that were missing this stunning sight. The snow-covered mountains surrounded by baby-blue skies were awe-inspiring. From my high perspective, I couldn't tell where the mountain ridge begins and ends. All of the peaks and valleys of the mountains appear to flow into each other and blanket the horizon. The jagged peaks are softened by the snowcaps and ribbons of blue waters winding around their base. The mountains fit together seamlessly. Only one peak, Mount Rainier, stands above the rest. Like a range of creative experiences that weave themselves through our life, sometimes we can spot an idea worthy of climbing, but all of the peaks and valleys are a part of us. The end product may someday look magnificent like Mount Rainier, but never without the backdrop of the process that led the way.

Get Busy Living or Get Busy Dying

My favorite film is *The Shawshank Redemption*. It's the 1940s fictional story of Andy Dufresne, a young and successful banker whose life drastically changes when he is wrongfully sentenced to life imprisonment for the murder of his wife and her secret lover. His time at Shawshank Prison is one of disgust and struggle but, ultimately, Dufresne's spirit of hope and friendship is too large to be caged. The Andy Dufresne character (masterfully played by Tim Robbins) is perhaps my favorite fictional character. His calm, steady nature, sharp intellect, ability to find beauty and joy in each moment, his genuine friendship with Red (played by Morgan Freeman) and passion to inspire those around him with hope are just a few of the traits I admire.

Unlike many of his cohorts in Shawshank Prison, Dufresne is continually creating. Whether he knows it consciously or not, he lives every day with an ethic of creativity. While some just sit and wait out their sentence, he uses his time in "the security line wait" of his life to create projects that exercise his gifts, expand his world, and impact those around him. He carves his own miniature chess board from soap stone, writes letters in support of his vision to expand the prison library, tutors another inmate to receive his G.E.D., performs tax returns for nearly every guard at Shawshank, and, oh yeah, develops a strategic plan to escape prison and bring down the crooked warden.

The Dufresne character is more than just the guy who teaches us how to break out of prison, dream, and live with contagious hope; his character reminds us of the power of an ethic of creativity. Ideas feed one another, and every experience and skill gained along the way prepares us for the time it comes to break out of our normal routines. Dufresne's normal routine just happened to be prison. When the time arrives to jump on an emerging idea, we remember his final words: "Get busy living or get busy dying." Dufresne's Mount Rainier was escaping prison. What will your Mount Rainier be?

Michael Ray, professor of the famed Creativity Course at Stanford University's Graduate School of Business and author of the book *The Highest Goal*, urges us to become what he calls a generative leader.

> "Consider the way in which a natural system regenerates itself. In a rain forest, for example, every living organism contributes to the ecosystem. Barring human interference, the rain forest is

regenerative. It never depletes its resources because every creature and every bit of vegetation contributes to the system; the forest recycles and flourishes on its own waste products. God has given us this model and this gift. When you are generative, you contribute to this cycle of renewal. Your synergy, something more than the sum of its parts, starts a positive spiral of intelligent growth. This is what life is all about: It is living with the highest goal. To be of service and make the contribution only you can make to the universe, you must become a generative leader - no matter what your role in life. You can be a leader to yourself, to one other person or to the world. But if you start right now with an intention of being generative, of letting your creativity create creativity around you, of giving and receiving, you'll see remarkable things happen."

We all have creativity flowing within us. We just have to take the time to listen to the essence inside us. Stimulating creative moments in your own life can begin by consciously deciding to do the little things in life differently. It starts with a willingness to step outside your comfort zone and approach your most routine tasks from a different angle of vision. As an exercise, try re-arranging the order of the way you begin your day, take a different route to work, pick a new spot for lunch, spend a couple of minutes searching for a subject online you know nothing about, or spend your evening free of the normal routine of dinner, TV, crossword puzzle, bed. We cling to our routines because it brings stability to the changes we experience around us. We hover around the baggage claim because that is the status quo. However, training our brains to see more options or solutions to every situation allows us to meet each new change with creative possibilities rather than complacency.

In organizations I've worked with, I've witnessed tremendous value that comes from teams that commit to "Step Back" visioning retreats. Finding space away from that crowded baggage claim as a staff, and entering into a dynamic, creative process, infuses new energy, new possibilities, and new collaboration. It's often in those spaces where true innovation emerges.

Put Your Shoes On First

My son Will, three years old at the time, walked up to me one morning while I was getting dressed for a meeting. All forty-two inches of him stood at my side and his giant blue eyes stared up at me. I had my underwear, shirt and socks on, and was beginning to put my pants on when he questioned my mode of operation.

"Daddy, why don't you put your shoes on first?" he said in his usual inquisitive way.

"Well, I can't put my shoes on before I put my pants on," I responded playfully. "You silly, everybody knows that if you put your shoes on first then you won't be able to get your pants over them. So, that's why you have to put your pants on first."

"Just try," he urged.

I knew this was a father–son moment, a teachable moment. I knew I needed to value his ideas, slow down, and take the time to be present with him. So, I decided to play along and show him. I slid my pants back off, put my shoes on, and then began to attempt to put my pants on. Sure enough, my pants slid right over the top of my shoes easily.

"See, I was right," he declared with a huge smile.

It was a teachable moment, and I took note. I decided in that moment that I want to be someone who puts his shoes on first in life. I want to be someone who continues to be willing to walk down the unconventional paths of life. Trying the option of putting our shoes on first is a powerful image for all the things we think we have figured out in life. Just as we think it is crazy to try to put our shoes on before our pants, we have to remember to try. Every challenge in this world has more than one solution. Every moment in our lives has more than one opportunity.

There is opportunity right now that surrounds you and your business, but you'll never see it until you take the time to *put your shoes on first.*

Next time you are sitting with *SkyMall* magazine in hand, don't just giggle at the outrageous products or fantasize about owning the lavish items. Instead, see it as a greeting card of creativity inviting you to let your mind wander. Allow it to give you permission to spend time on your wildest ideas, declaring value in your every thought—even the incomplete ones. Let this discipline of creativity flow beyond your airplane seat and permeate your daily life back home. Let it invigorate your work so that you can see possibilities rather than limitations. Allow yourself to see the most routine moments of your day differently and be willing to consider the unconventional paths of life as well. Become someone who lives an ethic of creativity!

Questions For Your Journey . . .
Embracing Creativity in Your Organization

I'm not sure why it took so long for someone to come up with the idea that a ketchup bottle could be reoriented so the open end is at the bottom of the bottle. For years, people shook the glass bottle, hit the bottom, smacked the little "Heinz 57" logo, or whatever strategy they subscribed to, in order to get the ketchup to flow toward the opening. Everyone just watched and followed the way the person in front of them approached this frustrating task. Finally, someone in the bottling industry asked the brilliant question, "Why don't we just turn the bottle upside down and let gravity do its work?"

Questions like that are ready to be asked at this very moment in your organization, personal life, and family. Asking "why?" is one of the most important questions to carry with you on your journey. Why are you doing what you're doing? What is the purpose for the event, product, or service that you are trying to plan? Why are you allocating the time, money, or energy the way you are? What if you and your organization chose to step back and look at your efforts differently? Are we meeting the expectations of our Mission and Vision with efficiency and productivity? How are we choosing to move throughout the world while we carry out our business?

*Creating an **ethic of creativity** is about inviting continuous questions, celebrating ideas, and having the willingness to try things differently. Allow time today for your thoughts to wander, for questions to rise, for the courage to try things differently, and the patience to let ideas evolve. Start with your personal process and then consider what it would look like to expand an ethic of creativity within your organization. Slowly, your actions and intentions will impact the way your organization moves throughout the world.*

- *I will spend fifteen minutes today thinking about a crazy idea I've had lately. I won't demand closure, but will allow the idea to wander like bamboo. Take good notes.*
- *What are the most creative moments I've experienced in my career so far?*
- *What ideas/experiences in my past helped lead me to those moments?*
- *Describe the environment(s) at work where I feel most creative.*
- *What question is needed to be asked right now on my team or in my organization?*
- *In what way(s) can I put my shoes on first today?*

Embrace SkyMall
Celebrate an Ethic of Creativity

Notes

"Creativity Is An Ethic."

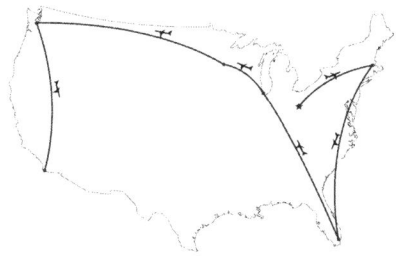

"*Leadership is character in action.*" - *Warren Bennis*

Take Flight

THE MINNEAPOLIS AND SEATTLE AIRPORTS ARE UNIQUE. Minneapolis' wood decor, string of upscale shops and various eateries, and a woman playing the harp in the corner made me question whether people actually want to leave the airport during Minnesota winters. The high glass windows in Seattle provide a clear view of the mountains in the distance. Coffee kiosks, elegant shops, food options outside the normal fast-food expresses, and comfortable places to sit are thoughtfully arranged throughout. The environment in both cities assists in creating a vibe that noticeably rubs off on travelers in calming ways. We're making progress.

Sitting by one of the windows in Seattle and watching a plane at close distance take flight is an impressive sight. I'm still baffled by the quick rate of speed attained by such a large metal object, which then gracefully lifts into the air. Years ago, I had a conversation with some friends in which we were listing all of the things we admittedly had no idea of how they work. Educated people surrounded by routine objects, but not sure exactly how they work. They work and you are glad they do, but you just haven't understood, or taken the time to understand, how. The microwave, satellite television, cruise ships that look like cities floating on the water and, of course, how airplanes fly.

Maybe we were absent the day they taught physics in school, but it was hilarious to listen to educated people fumble over the concept of flight. I was reminded of that conversation as plane after plane raced down the runway in Seattle and gently lifted into the air right before my eyes. So, I figured, at age thirty-two, it was time for me to do a little bit of research to quench this lingering thirst for knowledge. Shortly into my search, I realized that my perplexed friends and I were not alone in our lack of knowledge about airplanes taking flight. In fact, even within the world of physicists, mathematicians, and aeronautical engineers, there are many web sites debating the correct theories and rules of physics as they apply to flight.

So, I'm sorry if I offend anyone with my elementary understanding or approach to this topic, but I'm sticking with NASA's description. NASA's web site states that when a plane is sitting still, the pressure between gravity and the air is equal all around the plane so it stays right where it is. Makes sense. The key to how planes take flight, they say, lies in Bernoulli's Principle, named for Daniel Bernoulli, a Swiss physicist and mathematician who discovered this principle in the eighteenth century. The principle states: "Air moving over a longer path has less pressure than the same volume of air moving over a shorter path." Because the wings of a plane are curved differently on the top and bottom, when the plane gets moving at a high rate of speed, the air going over the top of the wing is stretched over a longer distance. Therefore, based on Bernoulli's Principle, the air moving underneath the wings, on a shorter path, creates more pressure and lifts the plane into the air. Simply put, that is how planes take flight. Now, that is certainly helpful and does make more sense, but I still think I would have been a little nervous to trust that theory the first time someone tried. I'm glad they tried.

Staring out the window again at the planes around me lifting into the air, I can't help wondering whether Bernoulli's Principle translates into other areas of our lives.

Could the Bernoulli Principle apply beyond the world of physics? Could it pertain to the social sector and provide an image of how to get an idea off the ground? Could the very same principle that explains how an airplane lifts off of the ground speak to us about getting a social movement to take flight? What could take this book from a collection of observations regarding human behavior at the airport, and lift the message and intention behind these images into the collective consciousness of our world? How could this spirit spread throughout the collective consciousness of your business? How would it begin?

As I stated in the very first line of this book, I believe we can change the world. We can change the world because each one of us has the innate ability to expand our awareness, change our focus, and alter our daily interactions. I believe attention to the biggest problems in the world must begin with the smallest of actions and an intentionally compassionate spirit. In order for any change to come about in the world, it has to come from you and me —from each of us. Culture change begins with individual choices. The pressure underneath the wings has got to be greater than the pressure above the wings. Change isn't going to happen because someone high up, such as the President, puts forth a mandate that pressures everyone to bring more caring actions to our smallest interactions (although it does help if the President leads the way). We know that alone doesn't work. It can't come just because the airports decide to set another rule to govern our behavior. This isn't about setting more rules to keep us in line, but rather it is about raising the awareness and appreciation for all around us. Real change has to come from the ground up. Just like every single significant movement in the history of the world, everyday people like you and me can decide to change our behavior in our daily encounters. That's how it happens—one individual at a time, one small event at a time, each of us deciding to choose a different way that we want to move together in the world. Slowly the autopilot of the way we've always operated disengages and the newly created spirit of interaction becomes our new way to live.

I'm not suggesting the change will come easily. I know we'll still have the seemingly irresistible urge to grab our bags and dash down the aisle way at the sound of the airplane's ding, to instinctively stake our place in the human wall at the conveyer belt when claiming our bags, to be annoyed that our wait in the security line would have been shorter if we only had chosen a different path, to zone out and remain with the status quo, rather than diving into a bubbling creative process with no end in sight. And, of course, to take the easy way out and not acknowledge the passenger beside us who seems to be struggling with life. I know we have to *act* our way into a new way of thinking, and that takes commitment and time. But, if we're able to bring awareness and make just a few slight adjustments in the airports and on the airplanes in our lives, just think what it'll mean in the business meetings, coffee shops, malls, courtrooms, hospitals, and little league games when we have a more significant situation to handle! It starts small and, by my observations, I don't think we're really all that far off.

Smile

A woman named Amanda, probably in her late twenties, approached me in Chicago's O'Hare International Airport because she saw me watching the crowd and taking notes. I was leaning against one of the pillars at a three-way intersection where thousands of travelers were passing by. More people wearing phone headsets then you can imagine flashed down the hallway and then, like salmon swimming upstream, crossed through the oncoming traffic and down one of the other two corridors. She walked up and said she was intrigued by what I was doing and wanted to meet me. She had straight brown hair and a very down-to-earth look about her. We started a conversation about human interaction and the interesting ways people behave in the airport. She had studied psychology in college and was excited and affirming when I described in general my thoughts on the ways we interact in airports. Along this trip

I have tried to stay fairly aloof in my conversations with strangers in regard to what I'm doing so their behavior remains authentic. However, Amanda seemed to genuinely get it right away.

She shared a story she remembered from a psychology class. The story, or parable since I haven't had much luck authenticating it yet, is about a guy who writes a suicide note before walking across the Golden Gate Bridge in San Francisco. The note reads, "If you find this note and I am now dead, then it is because I walked clear across the bridge without anyone looking me directly in the eye. I made a pledge that I will not commit suicide if someone looks me in the eye." The man had jumped.

Fiction or nonfiction, the story is a striking endorsement for the power, both good and bad, that lies within our eyes, smile, and intention to connect with those we meet during the small encounters in life. It paints the horrific picture of the other end of the spectrum from what I am talking about, and suggests what can happen when we don't act. Amanda was right that this story fit well with what I was doing. At each of the stops on my seven-day, seven-city airport adventure, I had been keeping some casual statistics along the way. I wanted to observe the mood, demeanor and manners of the public at the airport so that I could understand what kind of change we are up against. Two informal studies were born: (1) The Security

Line Study and (2) The Smiling Study (I'll think of more creative names during my first think tank).

First, the Security Line Study. I had two main preconceptions regarding the security line checkpoints. My original hypothesis was that most people are annoyed, frustrated, and upset after they come through the security lines. In my head, I had images of the majority of people griping and moaning as they grabbed the items they had shed for the x-ray machine, fumbling to re-assemble their possessions. My second hypothesis was that a very high percentage of people were being searched in addition to going through the x-ray machine (only adding to their chipper mood). In Boston, Miami, Minneapolis, Seattle, and Columbus, I sat on the gate-side of the security line checkpoints and observed one line only for thirty minutes. I tallied how many males and how many females came through the x-ray machines in those thirty minutes and, of those people, how many were additionally searched. The other observation I tallied was each individual's demeanor as they exited the checkpoint. I made a mark if they were smiling, laughing or looked noticeably happy. I made a mark if they were complaining, rolling their eyes in frustration, or just noticeably upset. Lastly, I made a mark if their facial expression was neutral, meaning they didn't appear to feel one way or another.

I learned that my pre-conceived notions were dead wrong. Of the 181 people I watched move through checkpoints in those particular airports, only eighteen were additionally searched by security—a lowly 9 percent. And, more significantly, only a whopping two of them looked upset. Yes, only two! That's 1.1 percent. By comparison, though, only four looked happy. Yes, four. That's 2.2 percent. So, what did all this mean? To me, it was an overwhelming slap in the face that we are on autopilot even more than I thought. We are walking around in neutral. We're not sad, but we're not necessarily happy. We're not outwardly upset, but we're also not necessarily smiling. We're operating in neutral; the autopilot is on. So, getting the concept of this book to take flight in people's lives doesn't appear to involve convincing us to move in an entirely new direction; instead, it's asking us to just turn our autopilots off and move slightly north of neutral.

Now, the Smiling Study. In her October 24, 2007, article "What's in a Smile?" Kimberly Read wrote:

> In psychology, there is a theory entitled the 'facial feedback' hypothesis. This hypothesis states that 'involuntary facial movements provide sufficient peripheral information to drive emotional experience' (Bernstein et al., 2000). Davis and Palladino explain that 'feedback from facial expression affects emotional expression and

behavior' (2000). In simple terms, you may actually be able to improve your mood by simply smiling!

This is not the first time that we have heard of the health benefits, mood alterations, and contagion of smiling. I decided to take that information and see how many people would respond to my smiles. How many people would smile back and how many would just remain in their autopilot trance? In the Boston, Chicago (O'Hare), Minneapolis, Seattle, San Diego, and Columbus airports, I walked the terminals for thirty minutes doing nothing but looking people in the eyes and smiling. Here were the only tally criteria: They had to make direct eye contact with me; there could be no verbal cues on my part; and they couldn't already be smiling. So, I smiled; and this is what I found.

Seventy-five percent of the people I came into contact with in those six thirty-minute studies smiled back at me. Of the 174 at which I smiled, 131 smiled back (75 percent). The others just continued along their way. For those interested, Seattle scored the highest, with 81 percent smiling back, while Boston and Chicago tied for the lowest, with 70 percent. The hardest part of this entire experiment seemed to be getting people to look me in the eyes—additional confirmation that our autopilot trances are so often concentrated on our own world that we're oblivious to what's happening around us.

Still, 75 percent on average–three of every four people-responded by moving from neutral into a smile. I choose to see that as a huge positive. Of every four people we come into contact with, we can impact the world for three of them just by smiling, even for just an instant—spreading joy quietly. This was great confirmation of the basic premise of this book and great hope for all those in the world who strive to make even the smallest of differences.

Messages of Water

Dr. Masuru Emoto is a Japanese researcher famous for his *Messages of Water* books first published in 1999 and for his spotlight in the documentary *What the Bleep Do We Know?* His highly controversial, yet mind-blowing, contention is that he found conclusive evidence that human vibrations such as words, thoughts, prayer, and music affect the molecular structure of water. In his experiments, Emoto says the use of a powerful microscope and camera allows him to photograph, before and after, the changes in the water crystals. Water samples assigned words such as "joy," "peace," and "thank you" show up as bright, sparkling images. The water samples given words like "death," or phrases like "you make me sick" show up as dark, ugly pictures. The water isn't just temporarily altered, according to Emoto, it is changed.

In Reiko Myamoto Dewey's interviews with Emoto entitled *More Messages in Water*, Dewey wondered if this water truly could be changed; could certain words actually be used to affect water for environmental purposes?

"Have you come across a particular word or phrase in your research that you have found to be most helpful in cleaning up the natural waters of the world?" Dewey questioned.

Yes. There is a special combination that seems to be perfect for this, which is *love* plus the combination of thanks and appreciation reflected in the English word *gratitude*. Just one of these is not enough. Love needs to be based in gratitude, and gratitude needs to be based in love. These two words together create the most important vibration. *Love* is an active word and *gratitude* is passive. When you think of gratitude—a combination of appreciation and thankfulness—there is an apologetic quality. The Japanese word for gratitude is *kan-sha*, consisting of two Chinese characters: *kan*, which means feeling, and *sha*, apology. It's coming from a reverential space, taking a step or two back. I believe that love coming from this space is optimal love, and may even lead to an end to the wars and conflicts in the world. *Kan-sha* is inherent in the substance H_2O — an essential element for life.

His message leads to the central question, "What does all this mean if 70 percent of our bodies are water and 70 percent of the planet is made up of water?" Our thoughts, words, intentions, and vitality of our spirit impact us both internally and externally. Our intentions and spirit do impact the world we live in, at the smallest molecular level as well as in significant life events. Knowing that and putting it into action so that it takes flight in our lives are two separate things. Stepping back at the baggage claim, slowing down at the sound of the ding, embracing creative moments intentionally, and appreciating the zigs and zags of our life's path will enable us to put those loving and grateful vibrations into action all over the world. If we need a place to practice this spirit, then we should start at the airport and then carry it with us on each leg of our life journey. Our leadership vibrations do matter. Those little encounters won't just affect the world, but will change it.

Successful businessperson and speaker, Zig Ziglar said, "It is your attitude, not your aptitude, that determines your altitude." How many days do we walk through the front door of our work with a negative attitude? How often do we find ourselves functioning on autopilot as we move from task to task or meeting to meeting? Even those actions send ripples out into the world. Just imagine what it would mean to the quality of our work, our own mental well-being, and the culture of our team, if we could put ripples of a different spirit into motion.

A good friend and former colleague refers to it as "faithing." Faithing is taking the beliefs that we have at our core, the words we speak, the feelings we experience, putting it all together, and making it a verb—putting it into motion. It's one thing to say you love someone, but until those words are accompanied by action, they are insignificant. We spend so much of our lives discussing what it is we believe about this subject and that subject and what we think ought to be done about this or that (sound familiar for your organization?); but in the end, the only truly valuable contribution is what we're willing to do about it. What are you willing to do to bring your core beliefs, the words you speak, and the feelings you experience to life? Is your personal doctrine, moral compass or religious belief reflected in your daily actions? Are you willing to make the nice words you speak become an active reality in the world? Are you ready to go "faithing"?

Travel Gracefully

I remember watching her move through the security checkpoint in Boston. She appeared to be in her early-thirties. She was thin with dark hair and a simple, yet fashionable look. She was one of the very few chosen to have her bags searched at the security checkpoint. I watched as the fifty-year-old TSA security worker pulled her aside and slung her bag up on the counter. He unzipped it and began rifling through everything. He flipped her nicely folded clothes over and over, pulled her personal items such as underwear out into the open where anyone near could see, and asked the necessary, but ridiculous, normal questions about whether someone else had packed her bag for her. Her reactions were so authentic and graceful.

Throughout the entire search, she didn't show one moment of frustration, one ounce of annoyance. She spoke politely with the TSA guard, laughed at her own responses, and asked him questions about his day. When the search was finished, she took the disheveled bag and patiently reorganized its contents. One by one, people passed by her as she gathered her things. Just a few minutes later, she came running down the terminal hallway with her bag over her shoulder and a few remaining loose items draped in her arms. As she passed me, she yelled, "This isn't the easiest thing to do in heels" in the same gracious spirit she exuded at the checkpoint.

"I bet not," I yelled back. "But, you're doing it well!"

She was dashing toward her gate. She had obviously known she was running late when they were searching her bag, so why didn't she seem anxious? Why wasn't she annoyed that out of all the people in those security lines, she was the one they selected? Why wasn't she complaining about the way the man disrupted her perfectly organized bag? And, finally, with a long hallway to run in high heel shoes and a large, disorganized bag to carry, why was she doing it with such playful energy and joy?

I can't articulate anything about this woman's personal beliefs or speculate about what she thinks the solutions to the problems of the world are, but just by watching her, I could tell everything about the vitality of her spirit! Whether she knew it or not, she was *faithing,* she was putting love and gratitude into action, and it made an impact on me. The gracious and appreciative manner in which she handled each obstacle between herself and the gate was a lesson and model for us all. She was traveling gracefully through life. Like the wake from a passing boat on a lake, she sent positive ripples to everything along her path. After she passed me I found myself smiling, slowing down and feeling thankful for all the ripples around me. The mood along her path was changed. And just by watching her, my mood was changed. I moved from being a passive observer to wanting to be an active participant in the spreading of this spirit.

I think about the obstacles, delays and cancellations that show up along our path every day in life and business. I wonder how the cultures of the spaces we move in and out of could be changed by the ripples we create? The best leaders create infectious ripples along their path. Perhaps now it is time for us to travel gracefully.

Lift Off

The time in my journey had come. Seven airports in seven days, 10,000 minutes of observations at all four corners of the continental United States, and a lifetime of stockpiled traveling memories had been played out in my mind. I observed the small encounters of thousands of herded passengers in the crowded terminals of our airports, witnessed the incessant rush at the sound of every airplane's starter-pistol ding, chuckled at the comparison game at the security lines, been thrust into a creative process due to an airline seat that holds me still and a *SkyMall* that kick-starts wacky ideas, and experienced the significance of real-life happenings haunting passengers beneath their surface. So, finally, it was time for me to return to the baggage claim. It was time for me to return to the spot where this whole book was born. It was time for me to dive into the madness I've witnessed at every crowded baggage claim I've come into contact with in my life. It was time for me to step into the apparently self-serving, survival-of-the-fittest baggage-claim world and put my money where my mouth was. It was time for me to make the dream I have envisioned during those baggage claim experiences a reality. It was time, finally, for me to invite everyone to "step back from the baggage claim."

My heart raced as I anxiously approached the Terminal 2 baggage claim at San Diego's International Airport. There was the familiar scene of hundreds of people jam-packed around the conveyer belt, waiting for the bags to begin moving down the line. The mass of humanity was five or six rows deep at some turns of the conveyer belt. There were some families with young kids, high school and college students, young professionals, military personnel, what appeared to be high-level executives, and some elderly people probably in the final stages of their traveling lives. The gathering around this baggage claim was a true microcosm of the world many of us move in and out of every day. It was like the scene at the last convention you attended.

I paced around the outside of the mob of people, nervous to do what I knew had to be done. Just as the words would begin to creep up in my throat, I would step back to reevaluate. This wasn't my comfort zone. I didn't want to draw attention to myself. I wasn't sure if anyone would even listen or if I would just be the nutcase shouting in the corner. I didn't know what would happen in this age of TSA and heightened nerves at the airport due to terrorism. Would I get arrested or swarmed as soon as I began causing a stir?

At last, I knew I had to put my doubts aside and step out of my comfort zone. I knew this was the way my seven-day airport adventure had to end. The annoying buzzer to signal the movement of the bags had just gone off; it only elevated the frenzy of the crowd. The jockeying and elbowing at the conveyer belt had begun. It was time.

"Hey everybody," I shouted as I moved to a central place in the sea of people. "I've got a great idea. How about we all take three steps back so that everyone can see the conveyer belt? Then, when you see your luggage, go ahead and step forward to claim your bag."

People actually turned and listened. I had the crowd's full attention. Some got a kick out of my approach and began laughing. All were listening!

"Oh, and another thing," I continued in a humorous tone as I put my arm around the randomly picked middle-age woman in front of me. "If you happen to see this nice woman struggling to get her bag from the belt, why don't we go ahead and help her? Let's change the world!" I shouted.

The response was amazing! Everyone had turned and listened. I wasn't arrested! Some snapped out of their autopilot trance and actually began giggling with amusement. People at the front of the belt began looking at each other as if to see who would be the first to step back. A woman from near the front yelled back to me, "That's a great idea, but it'll never work!" Perfect! There's always a skeptic too afraid to try.

The most significant response, however, came from the very first person to respond to my plea. A young woman, probably in her late-twenties, standing only a few people in front of where I was standing, turned directly to me and said with a confident and extremely genuine tone, "Thank you. Finally, someone said it!"

I couldn't have been more excited as I exited the baggage claim area. I was bursting with affirmation. Not only had I moved through my nervousness and stepped outside my comfort zone, but the collective response from the crowd was perfect. I had impacted the entire mood around that baggage claim. Some laughed, of course one was skeptical, and the first words spoken were of gratitude, "Thank you. Finally, someone said it!" Perhaps I wasn't the only one who noticed the behaviors at the baggage claim, and was dying to yell that news from the mountaintop. Perhaps it just needed to be said and brought to the surface. Perhaps we just need to be invited to operate differently. Perhaps we all know, deep down, that we are better than our current mode of operation; that we want to bring a different spirit to the baggage claim in our lives!

So where do we go from here? Well, my declaration for my own life and my invitation to you for yours is simple. I'm committing myself to bringing a renewed spirit to the airport. No matter how much of a hurry I think I'm in, I'm going to reevaluate the importance of my so-called rush, and remember that the person on either side of me in the airport may actually be in a more significant hurry. Instead of fixating on the slow pace or frustration of the waiting game in the security lines, I'm going to find ways to enjoy where I am. I'm going to be more open to the people along my path who just may need someone to listen to them as they work through moments of suffering in their lives. I'm going to embrace the quiet moments an airplane seat offers us and allow creative thoughts to blossom. When the plane lands and the ding sends most into a frenzy, I'm going to sit still. And, lastly, when I approach the baggage claim, I'm going to stand at least three steps back so all can see and help those around me with their bags.

I'm committing to do these small things, and I invite you to do the same. In fact, I'm inviting us to carry this *Step Back from the Baggage Claim* spirit with us out the front doors of the airport and into our family lives, friendships, businesses, and common places of our world. This is a call to action. This is a call for us to move out of the comfort zone of past routines and into more inclusive and compassionate living. It is about teaching our eyes to see each day as a string of opportunities toward leaving our positive wake along the path we travel. It is a vision for how we can travel gracefully through daily life.

I invite you to share this with as many people as you feel moved to do so. We contribute to the cultures we want to create. Slowly, a movement can be born and a new mode of social interaction can lift off. Soon, this will become just the way we interact in the airports. This will be the new social norm for travel. If we can commit to these small adjustments in our lives at the airport, the same spirit of compassion and gratitude can't help but spill over to other, more significant, moments and spaces of our lives.

In our personal lives, faith communities, schools and businesses, we can use this metaphor to inspire more grateful, compassionate and creative actions. We can use this language to determine when it is time to *Step Back from the Baggage Claim* in our organizations and see things from a different angle of vision. We can use it to remind us to *Be Still* and remember our Purpose. We can use it to encourage us to be *Available* for those along our path. We can use it to live with gratitude right where we are *Now*. And lastly, we can use it to embrace an *Ethic of Creativity* and let it inspire us to put this leadership into action - allowing our strategies and visions to *Take Flight*.

As Jim Collins in his national bestseller *Good To Great* taught us, "Greatness is not a function of circumstance. Greatness, it turns out, is largely a matter of conscious choice, and discipline." True greatness isn't just about doing excellent things, but about creating excellent ripples. So, what kind of ripples will we consciously choose to create today? Around the metaphorical baggage claims in your leadership journey, what actions will you put into motion to positively impact the culture? In what ways will you invite your organization to examine not just "what" bags you are trying to claim, but "why" you are claiming them and "how" you are choosing to move throughout the world? There's someone in your organization right now dying to say, "Thank you. Finally, someone said it!" Be the change.

We can change the world. We can change the world because each one of us has the innate ability to expand our awareness, change our focus, and alter our daily interactions. We all have the ability to put powerful leadership actions into motion. We just have to start small and start where we are. Why not start to change the world by the way we live at the airport (or at the office)?

I'll meet you at the baggage claim!

Questions For Your Journey . . .
Taking Flight in Your Organization

*As you come to the end of this book, don't let the spirit of this movement end on the last page. Join those of us who have committed to carry these intentions with us on the next leg of our journeys. Change the world by choosing to travel gracefully, living this message not only in the airports, but throughout the path of your organizational life. Take time to step back and gain a new angle of vision and consider those around you. Slow down and commit to thoughtful excellence. Get out of the comparison game and into thriving where you are in the present moment. Embrace the creative process of living the life you want to live and, ultimately, build relationships and share compassion with those along your journey. Small loving actions in every facet of your life will change the world. Daily commitment to this spirit in all corners of our lives can't help but allow a movement like this to **take flight**!*

- *Describe the spirit and culture I hope takes flight in my organization.*
- *With whom will I share this movement?*
- *List 3 actions that I will bring to life in my work?*
- *How will I travel gracefully in our world today?*

Take Flight
Put a Grateful Spirit into Action

Notes

- *I will help share this movement by:*
  - *Traveling gracefully along my path*
  - *Sending a copy of this book to someone*
  - *Leaving a copy of this book with someone along the path I travel (and then track its movement around the world on our website . . . come see!)*
  - *Planning a Step Back retreat, team-building, or visioning session with my team*
  - *Connecting my organization to www.StepBackFromTheBaggageClaim.com*

Synopsis for the Baggage Claim in Your Organization...

- **Step Back** - *Step Back* from logistical thinking and begin with the question that must drive everything, "What is our mission and purpose for what we're doing?" Sounds simple, but a step that is often forgotten. When we are clear about our purpose and deeply rooted in "why" we do what we do, the "how" we choose to do it grows naturally out of the mission.

- **Be Still** - Commit time as individuals and as an organization to slow down and "Be Still". I guarantee it, you'll be better at what you do when you take time to reconnect, reflect, and refuel. It's counter-intuitive, but true.

- **Be Available** - Building relationships is the core of any successful entity. Call it networking. Call it team building. Or, just call it being human. When we drop our guard and allow ourselves to be *available* to those we sit next to on the airplanes, at the conference tables, or in the food courts, we open ourselves to authentic connections. It's a fact - when we connect with those we're "traveling with", we're better at what we do as a team.

- **Choose Now** - Don't let the obsession over 'Long Range Plans' get in the way of bringing excellence to life today. Get out of the comparison game and deliver the very best that you have to share with the world.

- **Embrace Creativity** - Make it a priority in your business culture to allow space where ideas are free to wander, grow, perhaps die, but always lead to something else. When innovative questioning becomes a part of your DNA, mid-flight corrections won't just seem possible, it'll become just the way you fly.

- **Take Flight** - You can't remain in *Step Back* mode forever. If you do, paralysis by analysis will set in and forward progress will be stymied. The point of all of this is to *Step Back* to gain perspective in the midst of a racing world, but then to put actions into motion that make a difference. The gauge of any successful endeavor is whether clear action items lead you to *take flight.* www.StepBackFromTheBaggageClaim.com

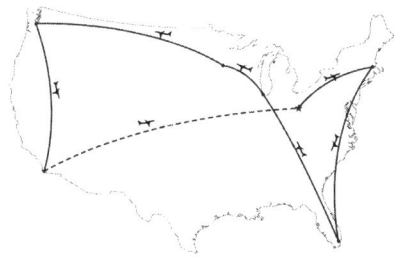

Step Back from the Baggage Claim

Change the World, Start at the Airport

Step Back
Gain Perspective and Create Space for Others

You Are Now Free to Move about the Cabin
Practice Stillness in This Moment

Ministry of Availability
Share Compassion with Those Along Your Journey

Choose Your Own Adventure
Quit the Comparison Game and Thrive Where You Are

Embrace *SkyMall*
Celebrate an Ethic of Creativity

Take Flight
Put Leadership Into Action

Step Back from the Baggage Claim

Seven Cities in Seven Days

<u>Frequently Asked Questions About My Airport Journey…</u>

- **Did you shower?**
    - No. Baby wipes and brief washings in the men's room did the trick.

- **Where did you sleep?**
    - <u>Sleep tally, 1/17/08–1/23/08:</u>

    1/17–18 – (Boston) 6 hrs 45 min
    1 hr on floor of Terminal B
    2 hrs in the chapel of Terminal C
    45 min on a bench
    3 hrs on floor of walkway
    1/19 – (Boston) 4 hrs 30 min
    1.5 hr on chair in food court
    1.5 hr on a bench
    1.5 hr on plane to MIA
    1/20 – (Miami) 3 hrs 45 min
    1.5 hr on floor of D Concourse
    45 min in chair
    1.5 hr on plane to CHI
    1/21 – (Minneapolis) 6 hrs 30 min
    5 hrs on wonderful bench on third level!
    30 min on flight back to CHI
    1 hr on flight to SEA
    1/22 – (Seattle) 5 hrs 45 min
    5 hrs on floor in ticketing area
    45 min on floor in ticketing area

    Total sleep on trip = 26 hrs 45 min
    Average = 4 hrs 45 min/night

- **What did you eat? Did you stick to twenty dollars per day?**
  - Yes; I came in under-budget.

Expenses on trip:
1/17 = $12
   $2.09 vitamin water
   $8.39 dinner (Chinese)
   $1.52 coffee
1/18 = $21.05
   $1.82 coffee
   $4.29 breakfast sandwich
   $1.82 coffee
   $3.77 lunch (pizza slice)
   $3.35 dinner (pizza slice)
   $6 beer & tip
1/19 = $16.56
   $1.83 coffee
   $4.40 lunch (chicken nuggets)
   $8.40 dinner (sandwich)
   $1.93 coffee
1/20 = $17.37
   $2.77 coffee + donut
   $8.08 lunch (burrito)
   $1.92 coffee
   $4.60 dinner (sandwich)
1/21 = $19.39
   $1.60 juice
   $5.40 lunch (burrito)
   $6 beer + tip
   $1.70 coffee
   $4.69 dinner (hamburger)

1/22 = $21.80
    $1.91 coffee
    $7.09 lunch (sandwich)
    $1.80 coffee
    $11.00 dinner (pasta)

1/23 = $8.70
    $1.91 coffee
    $6.79 lunch (sandwich)

Total airport expenses = $116.87
Average = $16.69/day

- **Since you obviously were sleep-deprived, what was one of the random thoughts you had along the way?**

    Top-10 List of "Interesting-Sounding Jobs I'd Like To Try For A Week":

    10. Plane deicer (They seem like a cool breed!)
    9. Bath & Body Works fragrance namer
    8. Chicken wing taster
    7. Practice dummy at a masseuse school
    6. Travel resort critic
    5. Fashion consultant for the band Flock of Seagulls
    4. Bungalow supervisor in Tahiti
    3. Violin liaison for Boyd Tinsley of the Dave Matthews Band
    2. Fortune cookie writer
    1. Pre-game speaker for The Ohio State Buckeyes football team

- **What were some other things you noticed about airports?**
    - Shoe shine stations still exist! And some people actually still use them.

    - Airports are not very energy efficient. From 2:30 to 4:30 a.m., nothing is open, but everything is still on. All lights are on, escalators continue to run, background music and automated announcements continue, and lights and computer screens at the ticketing counters remain on. With so many people carrying laptops, Ipods, cell phones, and PDAs on their travels, the need for power is in higher demand. An opportunity to conserve energy exists.

    - There are many people under thirty who travel. The opportunity for young people to experience the entire world is bigger than ever.

- **What else did you learn in the process?**
    - Time spent with no agenda is a great exercise. Being in a new environment with no clear agenda or time constraint was wonderful. I enjoyed slowing down, exploring, and letting my thoughts flow.

    - Carrying only the items you truly need is a liberating experience. It was great to be so mobile, flexible and able to be spontaneous in each moment because I wasn't bogged down with extra stuff.

- o I need a job. I stood behind a mother and her three kids at a Starbucks in Seattle's airport. Their order was one coffee, one hot cocoa and two cookies. The total cost was $9.96.

- o People are interesting. The more I talked with those around me and asked where they were headed, the more interested I became.

- **Besides the people you discussed in the book, who else made an impression on you?**
    - o There was a guy working a shoe shine station in Seattle. He sang a little jingle each time a prospective customer walked by his stand. He was having fun with his job and enjoying his wait in the "security line" of his day.

    - o Also in Seattle, I ended one of my nights sitting at a bar enjoying a beer. There were about ten people in the small pub. I watched as a long-haired man in his late-thirties sat in the corner playing his guitar. *American Idol* was on the TVs, and the small group inside the restaurant was all watching. Other than a few giggles at the *American Idol* judges' comments, the man contently strummed his guitar. Contestant after contestant performed on the screen. One of the contestants began to sing, and the man's head quickly swung toward the TV and he abruptly stopped strumming his guitar. He was mesmerized by the singer and began clapping as she ended her song. Watching an artist truly appreciate another person's talent was engaging.

- **Would you do it again?**
    - Absolutely!

Resources

Foreword
- Behar, Howard. *It's Not About The Coffee*. New York, New York. The Penguin Group, 2007, 2009.

A Note From the Author
- Dictionary.com. http://dictionary.reference.com/browse/process

Introduction
- "Frequently Asked Questions." National Air Traffic Controllers Association website. January 22, 2008. http://www.natca.org/.
- "Frequently Asked Questions." Transportation Security Association's website. January 22, 2008. http://www.tsa.gov. http://www.tsa.gov/research/screening_statistics.shtm
- Amor Ministries. http://www.amor.org.

Step Back
- Collins, James and Porras, Jerry. *Built to Last*. New York, New York. HarperCollins Publishers, 1994, 1997, 2002.
- Reagan, Ronald. Remarks at the Brandenburg Gate. June 12, 1987. http://www.reaganlibrary.com. http://www.reaganlibrary.com/reagan/speeches/wall.asp
- Nin, Anais. January 20, 2008. http://www.anaisnin.com. http://www.anaisnin.com/guestbook/
- Hesselbein, Frances. Leader to Leader Institute. December 22, 2006. http://www.mgmtquotes.com/author/Frances+Hesselbein/

You Are Now Free to Move About the Cabin
- Oxfam International. http://www.oxfam.org.
- Charity Navigator. http://www.charitynavigator.org.
- Southwest Airlines. http://www.southwest.com.
- Wing, Richard A. *The Space Between the Notes*. Mobil Alabama: HB Publications, 1994.
- Camp Akita. http://www.campakita.org.
- Greenleaf, Robert K. *Servant Leadership*. New York: Paulist Press, 1977.
- Behar, Howard. *It's Not About The Coffee*. New York, New York. The Penguin Group, 2007, 2009.
- Public Broadcasting Service. http://www.pbs.org. http://www.pbs.org/wgbh/nova/everest/lost

- Politz, Andy. http://www.everestspeakersbureau.com. http://www.everestspeakersbureau.com/andyp.htm.
- Emerson, Ralph Waldo. http://www.inspirationalspark.com/attitude-quotes.html

Seat 16 F: Ministry of Availability
- Gonzalez, Carmen and Jorge. Casa Hogar Sion Orphanage. http://www.casahogarsion.com.
- Madson, Patricia Ryan. *Improv Wisdom*. New York: Bell Tower, 2005.
- Blanchard, Kenneth and Johnson, Spencer. *The One Minute Manager*. New York, New York. Berkely Publishing Group, 1981, 1982, 1983.

Choose Your Own Adventure
- *Choose Your Own Adventure* Books. http://www.cyoa.com http://en.wikipedia.org/wiki/Choose_Your_Own_Adventure
- Gladwell, Malcolm. *Blink*. New York: Time Warner Book Group, 2005.
- *Streets Mission Project*. First Community Church. http://www.FCchurch.com.://www.fcchurch.com/templates/cusfcc/details.asp?id=27263&PID=174808
- Goetz, David L. *Death By Suburb*. New York: HarperCollins Publishers, 2006.
- *Life is Beautiful (La Vita è Bella)*. Directed by Roberto Benigni. New York: Miramax Films, 1997.
- Washington, Booker T. "Up From Slavery." 1901. 1895 Cotton States Exposition Address, Chapter 14.
- Emerson, Ralph Waldo. http://thinkexist.com/quotation/what_lies_behind_us_and_what_lies_before_us_are/10712.html

Embrace *SkyMall*
- *SkyMall Magazine*. http://www.skymall.com. Early Spring 2008 edition, p. 45, 75, 147, 1-800-SkyMall.
- The Hotdog Grill and Bun Warmer. http://www.skymall.com. http://www.skymall.com/shopping/detail.htm?pid=102557542&c=10474
- The ROM exercise product. http://www.fastexercise.com.
- Henry, Todd. "The Accidental Creative." http://www.accidentalcreative.com. Podcast #90.
- Roberts, Will. "Growing Bamboo," Cooperative Extension Service, The University of Georgia College of Agriculture and Environmental Sciences, Authored credit: Will Roberts, Conyers, Georgia. http://pubs.caes.uga.edu/caespubs/horticulture/GrowingBamboo.htm

- *The Shawshank Redemption*. Dir. Frank Darabont. Castle Rock Entertainment, 1994.
- Ray, Michael. *The Highest Goal*. San Francisco, CA. Berrett-Koehler Publishers, Inc., 2004, 2005.

Take Flight
- "How Do Planes Fly?." January 22, 2008. NASA Observatorium, http://www.nasa.gov. http://observe.arc.nasa.gov/nasa/exhibits/planes/planes_1a.html
- Read, Kimberly and Marcia Purse. "What's in a Smile?" for A*bout.com: Bipolar Disorder,* October 24, 2007. http://bipolar.about.com/cs/humor/a/000802_smile.htm (accessed January 22, 2008).
- Emoto, Masuro. *Messages of Water.* New York: Atria Books, 2001.
- Dewey, Reiko Myamoto. "More Messages in Water: The *Spirit of Ma'at* interviews Dr. Masaru Emoto." Vol. 2 (November 2000). http://www.spiritofmaat.com/archive/nov1/cwater.htm (accessed January 22, 2008).
- Ziglar, Zig. http://www.woopidoo.com/business_quotes/authors/zig-ziglar-quotes.htm
- Collins, Jim. *Good to Great and the Social Sectors* - a monograph to accompany Good to Great. www.jimcollins.com, 2005.

Share
Step Back from the Baggage Claim
In Your Organization:

- Visit www.StepBackFromTheBaggageClaim.com
- Invite your organization to embrace a *Step Back* culture - pass copies with your staff and have Jason visit for a keynote speech or leadership development series. Learn more at StepBackFromTheBaggageClaim.com
- Utilize the online resources and video programs for your team or your individual leadership journey
- Sign-Up for the free monthly e-Newsletter on the site
- Follow on Twitter *@StepBackBook* *@JasonVBarger*
- Find on Facebook & LinkedIn
- Pass this book to someone along your path and share the *Step Back* spirit today in the world!

Need Discounted Bulk Copies For Your Staff?

Contact us directly:
info@stepbackfromthebaggageclaim.com

Does Your Team And Organization Practice

21st Century Leadership?

The 7 Key Attributes For Success

<u>Are You A?</u>

Servant Leader

Storyteller

Collaborator

Innovator

Daredevil

Adaptable

Global Citizen

Visit www.StepBackFromTheBaggageClaim.com
and let us begin the conversation with your team!

Jason Barger

Before taking off to sleep in airports and observe human behavior, Jason Barger led 1,700 people to construct 125 houses internationally for families living in poverty. He also implemented the *Streets Mission Project* to serve the homeless on the streets of Columbus, Ohio. As the former director of First Community Church's *Camp Akita*, he designed programming focused on living with joy, love, compassion, faith, and service for over 1,900 campers per summer.

Jason is a graduate of Denison University, where he served as Captain of the men's basketball team, and then received certification from Georgetown University in Nonprofit Executive Management. In 2004, he was one of five people in Columbus, Ohio, to receive a Jefferson Award, a national award given to "ordinary people doing extraordinary things."

Today, Jason, his wife Amy, and their children, Will, Benton and Brooke, live in Columbus, Ohio. As founder of Step Back Leadership Consulting LLC, Jason adds value to organizations through keynote speeches, workshops, creative 'Think Tanks' and visioning sessions, one on one coaching, and ongoing consulting. He is a sought-after speaker and consultant worldwide.

To learn more, visit StepBackFromTheBaggageClaim.com or www.JasonVBarger.com. Jason and Step Back Leadership Consulting LLC would love to add value to your organization.

Spread This Book Around the World!

1. Write your name and today's date below (add yours below if you're not the first name).
2. Leave this book with someone along your traveling path.
3. Visit www.StepBackFromTheBaggageClaim.com and enter the first owner's name/date that appears below and your information.
4. Log back in to the site to see where your book travels!

First owner's name & today's date: _____

Example: Keith Byars 9/18/10

City where book was left: _____

Next to Spread the Book:

Name & today's date: City found: City left:

Travel Gracefully.